MW01533413

THE MICROWAVE GOURMET
Incredible Gourmet Meals
You can Cook in a Microwave

Jonathan Greene

Washington
County

November 2016
WASHINGTON COUNTY LIBRARY
8595 Central Park Place • Woodbury, MN 55125

THE MICROWAVE GOURMET

Incredible Gourmet Meals
You can Cook in a Microwave

Copyright 2015 Jonathan Greene

All rights reserved. No part of this publication may be reproduced in any form or by any electronic or mechanical means, including information storage, photocopying, recording, and (or) any retrieval systems, without permission in writing from the publisher, except by a reviewer who may quote brief passages in review.

This book is not meant to cook for you. Please make sure you cook foods completely and pay attention to any potential food allergies that you or your guests might have before serving food. Killing grandma doesn't make for a great after dinner story! Please use microwave-safe plates and bowls, or glass when you have a chance.

This book is dedicated to Natalie, because she still believes that microwaves use nuclear radiation and toxic waste to cook food like some crashed alien spaceship, no matter how many times I explain microwaves to her.

About Jonathan Greene

Jonathan Greene is a Freelance writer who worked in the Food Service industry as well as spending time with several restaurant Entrepreneurs in the Northern California.

He now splits his time between Los Angeles, and New York where he works with start-ups and newly formed businesses to connect to industry partners and restaurateurs. This man knows how to 'throw-down' with a microwave.

Other titles you may be interested in!

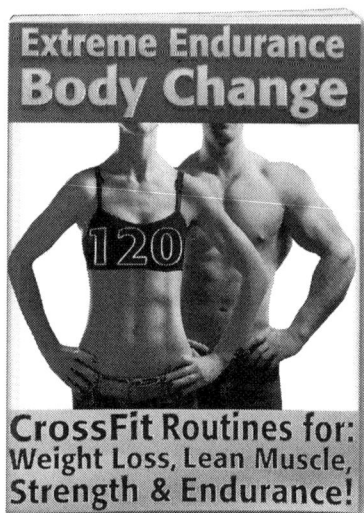

Extreme Endurance Body Change
120 of the most grueling workouts you can imagine. This Book takes you from novice to expert in as little as 4 short months! Achieve your personal goals quick, and at your own pace!

This book literally has every single workout ready for you to begin and space to record your progress.

_____

Mental Training: *The Art of Life or Death Decision Making*

Learn how to focus your mind and conquer fear so that you can make life or death decisions with confidence! **This book could literally save your life!**

Best Selling Author Nicholas Black takes you to the brink of death and teaches you what to do when there is no second chance.

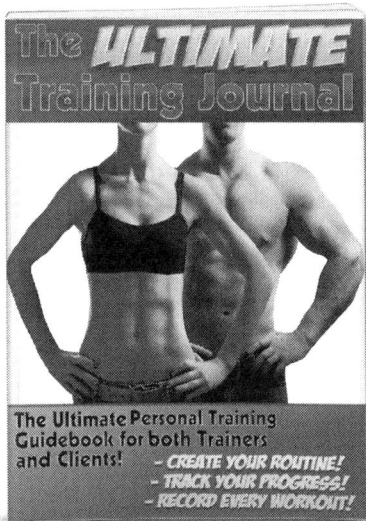

The Ultimate Personal Training Guidebook for both Trainers and Clients!
- CREATE YOUR ROUTINE!
- TRACK YOUR PROGRESS!
- RECORD EVERY WORKOUT!

The Ultimate Training Journal

This is the perfect training book and journal for both trainers and Personal Training Clients. It educates the clients, while at the same time being a wonderful daily tracker with advice and logbook pages to record and structure 16 weeks worth of workouts including all body measurements!

Contents

Desserts

FREE Previews!

Free Book Previews!

Who says reading a book isn't as fun as being at the movies?

Here is a look at some of our other titles. If you find anything that interest you, great! If not, jumping ahead to the start of the book.

Now, depending on your tastes you might want something a little edgy, or scary, or just cerebral. We find our readers are typically discerning, intelligent, and witty. Most of our readers email us or give us feedback, and believe it or not, that does affect the projects we work on. There are a couple of these novels that we're working on for television, and that has definitely been a strange and unique journey.

Right now, the following books are in various stages of production:

Nonfiction

- **Mental Training:** *The Art of Life or Death Decision Making!*

However strange and oddball this process is, we always try to return to our roots . . . a good, ole' fashioned typewriter—with a badass microphone and Dragon Dictation software so we can sit back, lazily drinking Dr. Pepper, telling a bunch of stories until we have grammatically vomited a book into existence.

Please, please, please, leave us review or email us with your thoughts or concerns. If something makes you angry, tell us. If you find something offensive or vulgar . . . that's pretty much par for the course. If you like our books, please pass them along to friends. If you hate our books, please buy 17 copies and use them in your fireplace over the winter. We won't get mad and we make great kindle-*ing*.

Without further ado . . . have some fun checking out the first few pages of a few of our titles!

Kindle**Unlimited**Exclusive

MENTAL TRAINING
THE ART OF LIFE OR DEATH DECISION MAKING

How to FOCUS
your MIND and
CONQUER
FEAR so that
you can make
life or death
decisions with
confidence!

Best Seller

By **NICHOLAS BLACK** *with* PHILLIP SCH...

★★★★★ ☑ (26)

#1 Best Seller in Sports Psychology

Introduction – Mental Training

Life is just a series of nightmares

In the dark you hear everything. Each step seemed loud enough to wake-up everyone in the house. And not just the people sleeping, but also the other things that scurried around outside the limited range of my senses. There was only a single, tired yellow nightlight to guide me from my room, down the hall, past the stairwell that led down into the darkness, and finally to the small bathroom. Each time my foot dropped to the carpet I could imagine things swimming in that blackness that swallowed the stairs.

Never look to the right on the way to the bathroom because, likely, something will be peering back up at you.

I would find safety in the bathroom, quickly easing the door closed behind me. I made my way to the sink throwing splashes of cold water on my face as I slurped to quench my thirst. I had limited visits to the bathroom in the night, due to the monsters and such, so I had to make the most of it. I would fill my stomach with water, use the bathroom as quietly as I could, and extinguish the light before I opened up the door again. Round two.

Never look to the left on the way back from the bathroom because whatever was watching you the first time has probably come up with a plan to get you.

Back down the hallway I'd go, footfalls as loud as hammers smashing beneath me, and once again finding the safety of my bedroom, as I closed the door behind me.

Every night it was the same thing. Every night the near paralyzing fear. Every night the nervousness and apprehension. Every night the rational embarrassment at the irrational fear I had of the darkness. The fear that consumed me to the point of nearly pissing in my pants each and every night of my childhood.

I wasn't just scared of the dark . . . it *owned* me. It controlled me completely from the moment the sun went down until the blackness relented to the aqua blue, and the monsters had to go to wherever they went as the sun rose.

And all of this fear and trepidation made me start to become angry with myself. Even as a small child I felt like a failure because this thing—the darkness—had taken control of half of my life. So I decided to take steps . . . literally.

I remember very clearly that it was wintertime in Texas, where I was living at this point. It was cold enough outside that the downstairs of the house was markedly cooler. Under the cover of the noisy air conditioner pumping out heat, I made my way out of the room and this time I turned right! In fact, I stopped, squinted into the cold dark void and sat down on the first step for nearly 5 minutes before pulling a 'freak-out' and racing to the safety of the bathroom.

The next night I made it 10 minutes.

A few nights later I did the unthinkable . . . I went down to the second step.

Then the third.

Then the fourth.

And a few weeks later, when I had desensitized myself and had worked my way about 5 or 6 steps down into the blackness, I realized that I was submerged in it. I was no longer the little boy standing by the safety of the dim yellow night-light. I had become something different.

I was one of them.

One of the 'things' in the darkness.

And this incredible feeling of calm washed through me. I realized that when I was completely in the dark, I had joined the monsters and goblins and creatures without names. I had simply changed my place, from the light to the dark, and suddenly, my fear was transformed into a new kind of courage.

In the darkness, I now knew, we were all on even footing. Me and all of the other things I'll never see—my irrational fears of the unknown—had come to an understanding. Those of us in the darkness can see those of you in the light, but not the other way around.

Conquering fear is not really possible. However, we can learn, with mental training and repetition, that we can channel our fears, put them in perspective, and get to a mind state that allows for competent decision-making based on the *real* dangers.

I hadn't been scared of the dark. I was scared of the unknown forces that made the darkness their home— unknown entities, which didn't exist. My fears were unwarranted because there were no real facts to support my phobia. Fear is a very natural thing, but it can easily paralyze us into panicked decision making . . . or no decision making at all. People freeze up in combat all the time and once the body stops responding, completely controlled by the fear, and then they're finished.

Conquering my fear of the dark taught me, even as a small child, that no fear was so powerful that it could control me. And I learned ways to cope in very difficult situations. I've had to make many life and death decisions, for a variety of oddball reasons, during my life.

In life or death decision-making scenarios, there's usually only a small list of possible outcomes that are positive. Time is not on your side. Luck doesn't exist. All you have is your training and experience to guide you. You either have one or the other—**Training** . . . or **Experience**. There is *no* middle ground.

If you *act*, instead of re-acting, you can raise the statistical. chances for your survival and the survival of those you intend to help.

A slow *reaction* significantly reduces your chances.

Inaction means you or they die.

My name is Nicholas Black, and I'm going to show you how to deal with fear, by showing you how we've dealt with it. I've been shot at, stabbed, stranded, left for dead, hunted, stalked, and overwhelmed. I'm not a guru or a master at anything in particular. But I've had good coaches. I've trained with the toughest and most astute observers of *success conditioning*, military strategy, unconventional warfare, sports hypnotherapy, Mixed-Martial Arts (MMA), and emergency response.

I was a bodyguard, a member of the Navy and the French Foreign Legion, a bouncer, and a fighter. I'm by no means a hero, but I'm a survivor. I've found a way, one way or another, to be here writing this sentence that you're reading at this very moment. Since I'm admittedly not exceptional at anything in particular, that should reassure you that the basic guidance I can offer you is actually useful. There is some merit in my words simply because I'm here to give you these words.

Our idea with this book is to give you tools you can use (IDLE CAR and OCD decision-making processes), right now, that improve your chances for survival by giving you a process and a mental game for dealing with life or death decision-making scenarios.

I'm going to use events that occurred to me personally, as well as situations that my closest friends and comrades experienced. I will walk you into situations we faced; situations that had limited choices due to circumstances beyond our control. Many of these decisions were life or death.

Our goal with this book isn't to tell you what to do in a life or death decision-making scenario. Rather, it's to prepare you mentally to make the best decisions you can when time isn't on your side. That's what we're all fighting for, isn't it . . . more time. More time to choose the right path, and more time to make the right decision.

The samurai used to say that **you should consider matters of little concern greatly, and matters of great concern lightly**. They meant that if you spend enough time considering the little things and seemingly insignificant details, then the larger obstacles and challenges are little more than just a bucket of little problems that your mind has already dealt with.

Notice that I didn't use the word '*problems*.' Our minds tend to defer decision-making when we assume there is a problem. However, throughout our lives we face challenges and obstacles, and constantly surpass them. Your mind is a muscle, and decision-making under fire is a skill. Talent can't be taught, but a skill can be. You should read this book with the goal of developing the skills necessary to make life or death decisions. Train your body and mind to assist you in this process, rather than getting in the way, as our bodies and chemistry all too often do.

We're going to provide you with a basic fundamental understanding of your body's biological. driving forces, and then look at examples and scenarios that relate to the subject matter we are studying. This book can be used as a resource for training your mind in a variety of ways. If you have particular issues that need to be dealt with, this book will have you training almost immediately. If you want a broad understanding of the underpinnings of Life or Death decision-making then you've also got the right book.

Along the way I'll bestow upon you some of the techniques taught to me by Dan—my close friend and mental coach. This is going to give us some insight into the decision-making processes that were instrumental in these different scenarios. What you will come away with, by studying some the life or death mental training techniques, are a series of tools you can employ in your everyday life.

You can read this book as a mental training guide, as an introduction into high-stress decision-making, or just as a list of odd and incredible life situations that you may learn from or relate to. Each person will take something different from this book.

Take the bits and pieces we offer, consider them carefully before drawing conclusions. Each of the stories was included for specific reasons. Try and let your conscious mind get out of the way for a while as you read through, and let your uncomplicated mind absorb. Think of the stories here as different colors in a large set of paints, each one alone might seem vacant, but together they can create a mélange of images, as infinite as your ability to imagine them.

With each chapter you'll find **MENTAL EXERCISE**s and **CHAPTER TAKEAWAY**s. These are different mental exercises you should practice both with the reading of the text as well as on your own. Practice these on a regular basis (*at least one exercise per day, and preferably one in the morning and one in the evening before you sleep*).

Hopefully you don't have to make lots of life or death decisions in your day-to-day life. But with this training you can develop confidence, coping mechanisms, and the underlying mental toughness that's necessary to make life or death decisions quickly and confidently, no matter what the situation.

If we can develop a host of small mental skills— teachable and repeatable in nature—that help us get into that state in which our conscious mind isn't cluttering the decision-making process, then we become extremely efficient in times of high stress.

This book is dedicated to creating an environment of no-mind, or quiet mind, where all the noise in the world is gone. In that present moment your emotions and thoughts won't get in the way of your abilities.

You will conquer your darkness.

You will control your fear.

Follow me, friends . . . into the darkness as we pursue the uncluttered mind.

The Philosophy of *'Training'*

The differences between training in the Navy, MMA, and the French Foreign Legion

Having experienced training in the U.S. Navy (Boot camp and Basic Underwater Demolition SEAL training) and then training in mixed martial arts (Brazilian Jiu-Jitsu & Thai-Boxing), which led to me eventually training in the French foreign Legion, I got to learn a lot about the art of "training" itself. To be clearer—the more different types of training I went through more I understood the basic concepts and constructs of training people.

In the Navy, training is focused on getting a group of people who are very dissimilar to work together for a common goal, and the concept of patriotism and service to your country is more or less the driving force.

Training in the mixed martial arts is focused on an individual's ability to feel comfortable whether he is kicking, punching, trapping, or grappling. When you fight, it's really just you in the ring/cage versus the other person. No more time for coaching once the fight starts, more than some minimal commentary and shouting from your corner (which you rarely actually hear unless you have a completely uncluttered mind).

Training in the French Foreign Legion is focused on getting a bunch of very different people (from different countries, with different religious beliefs, most of which have criminal backgrounds or affiliations with organized crime and/or terrorist organizations), to not murder each other during the training. If, by some stroke of absolute luck and genius, your company doesn't slit each other's throats throughout the training, then you will end up about 26 weeks later with a group of very capable soldiers.

Navy training (especially BUD/S) is about repetition, attention to detail, and following the direction of your superiors. It provides a basic understanding of the skills necessary to function as part of a large team, and the constant physically demanding nature of it produces proficient soldiers who can take an uncanny amount of pain and still conduct business.

MMA training is about technique, over and over, until you don't have to consciously think about what you're doing in a fight. It builds reactionary calm and control during the violence a fight offers. A good MMA fighter knows how to unclutter his mind during the ebbs and flows of the fight.

Legion Training is about sustained physical. and mental abuse, prolonged over 26 or 27 weeks of abysmal French weather that teaches so many skills that they're too numerous to mention . . . all of it while you're learning to speak French (which isn't an easy language to just pick-up). They push the 'service to France' angle a little bit, but mostly it's just making guys dangerous enough in so many areas that when the French Government lets us out of our cages, it's pretty much a nightmare for everyone involved.

The French government loves it because the Legion is technically a Private Military Company and operates autonomously. What typically happens is that the government will use the Legion and NATO missions, UN peacekeeping missions, and other less publicized engagements. They actually loan out the Legion's services for a fee, and every legionnaire on the ground represents a paycheck to the government of France.

Those are the basic differences in the training philosophies. But the concept of training is the same. You have a skill that must be coached in a way that your team can understand it, practice it, and get so good at it that they actually believe in it. The more training the team participates in, the less difficult the skills become. Instead of getting caught up on all the minor details and intricacies of the skills they are learning, the team forms confidence in both the skills they're learning as well as each other. The more confident they are with one another, the more they develop trust in themselves and in the techniques they are being taught.

Thus, good training is a self-fulfilling prophecy. The more you train this technique the better you will become. As you continue training and becoming better the technique becomes easier and there's less mental involvement in each tiny decision along the path. The less you have to think about, uncluttering your mind in the process, the more efficient you become. Techniques that were once difficult to complete become simpler and almost automatic. Then you can learn more complex techniques that make you more efficient and more dangerous and more effective. The more you practice the luckier you get.

Like we say over and over: you either have training or experience . . . Or some combination of the two. If you're untrained, you're probably going to get beaten-up or killed. There is no sense of fairness in the universe. If you are untrained and lack experience then most likely you will become some kind of statistic when life or death decision presents itself.

Book Preview: *Mental Training*

One of the very interesting things about this book is that you can learn from our collective pain and prepare yourself for a life or death situation. Little skills slowly coalesce into techniques, which your mind can anchor to various muscle movements. With repetition the• little skills fade away and become techniques.

By studying the techniques and their applications you can train your body to make very complex choices automatically, without thinking of all of those little bitty details you had to consider when you were learning all of those little skills.

One of the SEAL instructors used to explain it in the terms of a tree. When you first look at a tree you just see a tree. But if you break it down you start to see the bark, all of the branches, all of the tiny wrinkles and folds in the bark, the roots, and so many leaves that you can't even count them. But once you understand all of these little details you can step back and you just see a tree again. All of the little details become the tree.

Problem solving and decision-making are much like this. You can see all the little problems and focus on them, or you can have your mind clear and uncluttered, which allows you to see the entire challenge for what it is.

Your mindset for training should be inquisitive, open-minded, and without judgment. You must have your proverbial glass half empty so that you can learn new things. Even if you learn something that you feel is 90% nonsense . . . There is still 10% in there that could potentially save your life. Life and death decision making is about statistics and percentages, so if you can steal some technique here and borrow some technique from over there, pretty soon your mind and body are ready to deal with any situation because you've seen everything beforehand. Nothing will surprise you if you are trained.

Enjoy training.

Remember how you felt when you were a little kid and you first tried to play sports. For me it was soccer, and I was absolutely terrible at it. But I love the game so I practiced over and over until I got pretty good at it and then I found myself really enjoying competition because it felt as if the techniques came easier. And let's all be honest, it's really fun to win on a regular basis.

In a life or death scenario we want you to win. This process is not about *morality*, it is about *survival*. Long after you have been involved and surpassed a life or death decision you can look back on the ramifications of your actions. However, if your dead . . . I'm not sure how much Monday morning quarterbacking you can do.

In your mind you should look forward to training, especially mental training. Being a more efficient decision-maker and problem solver will help you, not just in a life or death scenario, but also in every aspect of your life. Our lives are just a long string of decisions.

From chapter to chapter we are going to present you with situations and scenarios that we believe are integral in developing a skilled decision-maker. Sometimes you will be the good guy, sometimes you will be the bad guy. On occasion you will be the Savior, and at other times the Grim Reaper. If you can concede the fact that most of us on this planet are reacting to forces far above and beyond our ability to control them then you are open-minded enough to become really good at life or death decision-making.

As we move forward:

Be the good guy!

Be the bad guy!

Be the sinner and the saint!

Be the silent operator who has a man between his crosshairs.

Be the paramedic who is covered in blood as he fights to keep a child alive.

Be all of these things as you read, and enjoy the ride. Enjoy the training and be as honest with yourself as possible.

This may be the most important book you ever read. Consider that statement. This might actually be the most important book you ever read.

Why?

Because the stories and techniques may save your life, or the lives of the people you hold most dear to you.

Now take a deep breath and lets learn how to breathe.

Breathing (Science Mumbo-Jumbo)

How important is Breathing?

We need to take a quick moment to talk about breathing before we get started. When an intense situation arises our bodies can become overwhelmed with emotions, with neurotransmitters and physiological changes, hyperventilation, anxiety, and other less obvious physical. changes. It's important to have a quick system that gets us out of that panic state, helping us to make decisions as well as to become calm and relaxed under normal circumstances.

Deep breathing stimulates our ***parasympathetic nervous system*** (**PNS**), which regulates body activities when we are at rest. It counteracts the ***sympathetic nervous system***, which triggers different body activities related to the *fight-or-flight* response.

Think of it like fire and ice: fire is the sympathetic nervous system, always on the verge of madness, crazy and overwhelming. Ice is the parasympathetic nervous system, calming and relaxed.

Breathing is one of the only functions in the human body that can actually be controlled externally through simple voluntary techniques. By making subtle changes to the rate, pattern of breathing, and depth of each breath we can change the messages that are being sent from the respiratory system to the brain.

Breathing exercises and techniques are like having a way to hack into the autonomic communication network. By doing so and changing our breathing patterns, we are sending very unique and specific messages to the brain in a way that it can interpret very simply. With these techniques we can convince the areas of the brain that are related to thought, behavior, and emotion to settle down and leave us in the best place to make life or death decisions.

From our research we have discovered three basic techniques for breathing control:

Coherent Breathing

>   **Coherent breathing** can be simplified to breathing at a rate of five breaths per minute, which falls right in the middle of the resonant breathing rate range. This is achieved by breathing in for a count of 5 to 6 seconds (inhale), and then breathing out for a count of 5 to 6 seconds (exhale).

- Coherent breathing causes shifts in the nervous system and cardiovascular system, which helps to create a stronger stress–response system.

Resistance Breathing

>   **Resistance breathing** is a form of breathing that creates a resistance to the flow of air entering and exiting your body.

This resistance can be created in a variety of ways:

- Pursing the lips
- Placing the tip of your tongue against the inside of the upper teeth, near the gums
- Tightening the throat muscles
- Partially closing the glottis

- Using external objects such as a straw or your own cupped hand
- Breathing out of your nose (which creates slightly more resistance than mouth breathing)
- Certain songs and chants (which contract vocal. cords slightly)

Breath Moving

Breath moving is a technique that is more mental than physical, where your imagination attempts to move your breath. The history of this technique dates back to the 11th century, when *Christian Orthodox Hesychast Monks* used to perform these techniques so that the Russian warriors could help to protect their territory and conquer their adversaries in battle.

We are a little bit less drastic in our use of breath moving, and feel there is a wonderful precursor to mental exercises and success conditioning.

Initially, you should start with 10 - 12 cycles of breath moving. In order to accomplish this technique (*which we would recommend for breath control in non-stress-related situations) you should follow these basic steps:

- While breathing in—imagine you are moving your breath to the top of your head, above your eyes.

- While slowly breathing out—imagine your breath flowing down into the base of your spine, towards your hips.

- With each cycle of breath in you should imagine the air going up into your head, and with each breath outward that air will make its way to the base of your spine.

When should you practice breathing techniques?

The simple answer is that **you should practice breathing techniques every single day** because your intention is to have these breathing techniques become second nature to you. These are tools that you will use to focus your breathing and your thoughts, calling your emotions, and preparing you to practice your success conditioning and reach your ideal performance state.

During times of great stress, trauma, and any life or death decision-making scenarios you will need to be able to quickly prepare yourself for whatever obstacles and challenges present themselves. That means getting your PNS working to control your crazy sympathetic nervous system before it crashes you!

Before any of the mental exercises that you will perform throughout this text, please choose one of the breathing techniques beforehand.

Introduction: *The Microwave Gourmet*

The Microwave Gourmet

The central concept behind the Microwave Gourmet was to develop a list of recipes that all of us could use in a pinch when we want a delicious meal, but are limited on time and materials. Cooking with microwaves is almost looked down upon by chefs and professionals in food preparation. People seem to have a predisposition to assume microwave food is fast and cheap... as if to prepare food in a microwave damns that food to be mediocre and unfulfilling.

We say, "You're just not cooking the right things!"

Well, we're about to change all that. These are some of the most tasteful and enjoyable recipes we have experimented with and we think you'll really appreciate both the flavor and effortlessness of them.

Will this book make you a food Genius? Perhaps it will. Will it give you decadent food weapons to use in a pinch?

Definitely!

So if you know somebody who doesn't respect the power and capabilities a microwave, take some of these recipes, create an incredible dinner and invite them over. Once they finish the meal, sitting back with glee and bliss you can tell them you made this entire meal in a microwave! You will reign as culinary king or queen among the people.

Here are just a few of the things you'll learn to prepare in short minutes:

- Risotto
- Enchiladas!
- Roasted garlic

Introduction: *The Truth about Microwaves*

- Sour cream and onion veggie chips
- Sweet potatoes
- Ropa Vieja
- Chicken & Dumplings
- Ratatouille
- Macaroni & Cheese
- Lemon-Horseradish Sole
- Loaded Baked Potato
- Salmon en Papillote
- Chicken Penne Al Fresco
- Fried Rice

Breakfast

- Egg whites and cheese breakfast sandwich
- French toast
- Scrambled eggs
- Bacon
- English muffins
- Mason jar pancakes

Desserts

- Toasted Nuts
- Baked Apples in a Bag
- Monkey Bread
- Cinnamon Roll
- Vegan Coffee Cake
- Granola
- Lemon bars
- Peanut brittle
- Mug cake
- Chocolate peanut butter mug cake
- Chocolate Chip Cookies

So let's begin!

The TRUTH about Microwaves

This seems to be a great deal of confusion surrounding the safety of microwaves, and what they're secretly doing to your food when you're not paying attention. We are going to dispel some of the myths and bad science that you'll frequently hear by people who have little or no real understanding of the basic physics involved in microwave ovens.

Myth: Microwaves use nuclear radiation to heat food!

The Truth: Microwave ovens use micro-waves at specifically set frequencies (somewhere between radio waves and infrared radiation on the electromagnetic spectrum, around 2,450 megahertz) to agitate (shake) water molecules in food.

The specific science is that this frequency range has an interesting affect in that the waves are absorbed by water, sugars, and fats. Once absorbed, they're converted directly into atomic motion – what we call heat.

Microwaves don't get absorbed by most plastics, glass, or ceramics. Metal reflects microwaves, which is why metal objects don't work well in a microwave oven and sometimes spark. Microwaves have metal walls to reflect back the microwaves into the interior of the machine, where your food is cooking.

As these water molecules get more and more agitated, they begin to vibrate at the atomic level and produce heat. The head that results is what actually cooks food in your microwave oven.

Introduction: *The Truth about Microwaves*

A conventional oven cooks by the **conduction** of heat, from the outside of the foot toward the middle, using hot, dry air, evaporating moisture (*which is why the outsides of food typically gets brown as you cook it in an oven*).

Microwave ovens use the microwaves to **excite** the water, sugar and fat molecules, so they basically cook each atom at the same time. Now, there are random unevenly thick or dense areas of food that may not cook perfectly uniformly (but this would be the same in a conventional oven).

The way that microwave popcorn bags and those little pizza plates work to crisp food is to use a bit of foil and cardboard so that they become very hot and that dries up those areas of the food, allowing the heat to brown and crisp the food.

Myth: Zapping food in a microwave leaches out key nutrients!

The Truth: If prepared correctly, cooking in the microwave is one of the best ways to retain your food's vitamins and minerals.

Essentially, the biggest threat from microwave cooking is that you burn the crap out of your hand, or use the wrong kind of plastics to cook with. Obviously, you wouldn't use plastics on an oven because they would melt and you could mix your food with chemicals in the plastics. Well, you also need to be sure you're cooking with microwave-safe plastics so that you don't gobble up plastic junk. Common sense, people.

Using a microwave with safe plastics is actually near the top of the list, nutritionally, for sound food-preparation methods. Using a small amount of water to essentially steam your food from the inside will retain more vitamins and minerals than almost any other cooking method.

- "Whenever you cook food, you'll have some loss of nutrients," says registered **dietician and certified food scientist Catherine Adams Hutt**. "The best cooking method for retaining nutrients is one that cooks quickly, exposes food to heat for the smallest amount of time and uses only a minimal amount of liquid."

Examples: 1. If you boil spinach on the stove it will lose up to 70% of its folic acid. Microwave it with a little water and you'll retain nearly ALL of its folic acid.

2. Cooking Bacon on a griddle until its crispy creates *nitrosamines* – which can **cause cancer**. Cooking the bacon in a microwave creates far fewer of these cancer-promoting chemicals.

Myth: Cooking food in a microwave can make you sick.

The Truth: If prepared with microwave-safe containers, covered tightly, with a minimal amount of liquid, it's actually more healthy than conventional cooking. In fact, using a microwave to cook can actually enhance the nutrition of some foods.

It makes the carotenoids in tomatoes and carrots more available to our bodies. It makes the biotin in eggs digestible so that our bodies can metabolize it. The intense heat kills bacteria in food that can make us sick.

Summary:

Well, now that we understand how microwaves actually work (by exciting fat, sugar, and water molecules) we see that they aren't dangerous at all. In fact, they're *more* healthy in most cases! So when people start giving you all of their 'flavor of the month' Men's Health arguments, shake your head and laugh manically. They're idiots, so let them be idiots while you cook your next incredible delight.

Now let's get to the good stuff!

Entrees

Risotto

This is one of my absolute favorite recipes for several reasons. Firstly, we are using a plug-in microwave to make risotto. Second, we are going to accomplish this in 10 minutes or less! We're not standing around the stove, stirring, making small talk, second-guessing our lives... We cook, we serve, and we take the praise. That's what we do!

Ingredients:

Essential/Basic Recipe

— 2 cups broth

Risotto

— 1 half onion which is finely chopped

— 2-garlic clove's that are finely chopped

— 1/2 cup of white wine (nothing too fancy)

— 1 cup Arborio rice (go cheap, it doesn't matter)

— 2 tablespoons of delicious butter

Different Varieties/Options

Mushrooms + Thyme

— Mushrooms

— Thyme

— Parmesan cheese

Butternut Squash + Sage

— Butternut squash

— Parmesan cheese

— Sage leaves

Bacon + Kale + Mushrooms

— Bacon, which you have cooked and crumbled into little bits

— Mushrooms

— Kale

— Parmesan cheese (we love this stuff)

Process

Once you understand the basic risotto recipe you can make dozens of different varieties of risotto. You will be able to add your mix-ins about halfway through this preparation process.

Each risotto is going to start with butter, onion, garlic, broth, and Arborio rice.

- **ORGANIC FOODS**: You may elect to use organic ingredients in as many places as you can, however you may be limited based on your local supermarket's availability.

Begin by adding **1/2 tablespoon of butter** to each ramekin (*a small dish for baking and serving individual portions of food*), and then add a **spoonful of diced onions**. You will microwave these four about 90 seconds on your high setting, stirring every 30 seconds to evenly distribute the butter.

- **Cooking Note**: Onions have a tendency to *spark* in the microwave, which can scare you! It's not *Al Qaeda*; so don't be alarmed! However, once they are covered with melted butter this should stop.

Now you need to add a pinch of **garlic**, along with **¼ cup of rice** and **¼ + 2 tablespoons of broth**. Different broths can create unique and interesting flavors, so definitely experiment.

You will want to cover your ramekin loosely with plastic wrap and heat in the microwave at **50% power level for 120 seconds**.

Remove the plastic coating and **stir as you add additional broth** (if the rice looks too dry). If you add additional broth, you will want to reheat, and check every 30 seconds.

Risotto

After heating for a total of 4 minutes (240 seconds) you can **add some of your white wine**. Try not to drink too much before you get to this point in the process! About **1 to 2 tablespoons of white wine per ramekin** should suffice.

You may now add your **butternut squash**, or **mushrooms**, depending on which recipe you elected. Cover the dish again with your plastic wrap and heat it for an additional **120 seconds at 50%** power level.

Risotto

If you are a glutton like we are, you've already started eating at this point and half of your wine bottle has been polished off, and you're going through your phone looking at ex-girlfriend's and ex-boyfriend's phone numbers. Look, but don't call. Just let it pass.

Anyway, let's go a little further.

If you are preparing the **Bacon + Kale + Mushroom** recipe to this risotto, you will want to **add your**

chopped bacon and kale at this point. Again, you will heat for another **60 seconds at 50%** of your microwaves power and then add your **Parmesan cheese**.

Now it's time to tell some lies about how long it took you to cook this meal!

If you find yourself standing next to a prison microwave while you prepare this food, have the satisfaction of knowing that even though you are presently incarcerated, nobody on the outside world is having a better meal than you. Obviously, if that is the case you will probably have to forgo the white wine option (*unless of course you have mastered the art of jailhouse hooch!*).

Risotto

If you are making the variety of risotto that includes **Mushrooms + Thyme**, you simply add your **thyme**, then heat for **60 seconds on 50%** of your microwaves available power, and as the delicious steam rises off of your dish you can add Parmesan cheese.

Risotto

Serve and enjoy like the king you are (*or queen, Caitlyn*). We don't judge the chef, only the cuisine!

Risotto

Enchiladas!

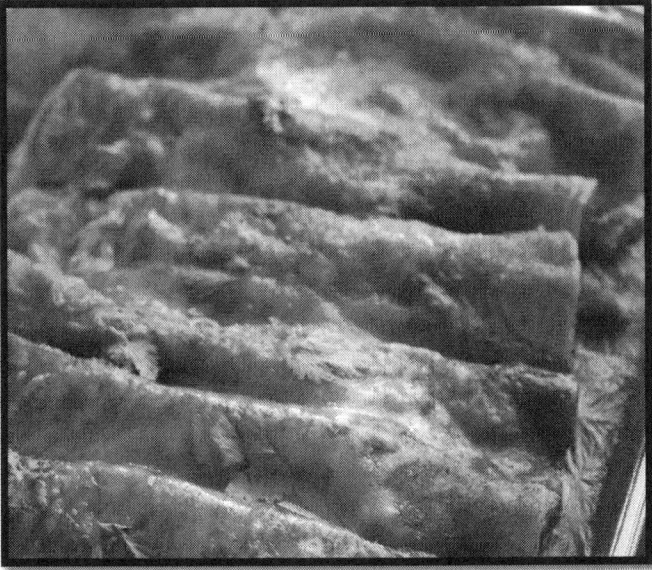

Enchiladas, in a microwave, in 10 minutes . . . are you kidding me right now! No, we are not kidding. This is serious grub with a distinctly Mexican twist. Can you say, "Caliente!"

Ingredients:

For the Enchiladas

- 12 corn tortillas (something fresh)
- 2½-3 cups enchilada sauce (see below)
- 2 cups of cooked chicken, it can be either shredded or diced

19

Enchiladas!

- 1 cup of cheese, preferably shredded (cheddar, Colby, Monterey jack, etc.)
- ½ cup of cilantro

For the Enchilada Sauce

- 2 teaspoons of ground cumin
- 2 teaspoons of garlic powder
- 2 teaspoons of onion powder
- 1 teaspoon of dried oregano
- 3 tablespoons of oil
- 3 tablespoons of gum-free gluten-free rice flour blend, (You can go gluten free or not, but I choose gluten free because it's basically designed by aliens and I can't support that)
- ¼ cup of red Chile powder
- Salt (to add taste and flavor)
- 1½ cups of chicken broth
- 1½ cups of water (not tap water if you live in Los Angeles, just saying)

Process

For the Sauce

We are going to **prepare the enchilada sauce first**, so that when we get to making the enchiladas themselves, you'll have everything ready to go.

Enchiladas!

In a saucepan **mix together all of the spices** we have included above (cumin, garlic, onion, oregano, etc.), the **flour**, and also the **oil** (hopefully olive oil). **Heat** this all together while **whisking for about about 3-5 minutes**, and you'll be ready when all of the floury taste and smell is gone.

While you're **continually whisking you need to add the chicken broth and water**. Keep whisking until the entire mass is smooth.

Keep heating all of this goo **until the sauce comes to a boil**, and then you are going to want to **simmer for 2–3 minutes** (120-180 seconds) or until the sauce is sufficiently thickened. Voila, you should have your sauce ready to go. **Keep it warm, on a low simmer** until its chow time.

Process

For the Enchiladas

For the first step in this delicious adventure you'll want to **heat up your tortillas for about 30 seconds** in a microwave. Just wrap them in a paper towel to hold a bit of moisture.

Next, you're going to **spread about ½ cup of your simmering enchilada sauce over the bottom of a**

Enchiladas!

9x13 glass (microwave safe) **pan**. You can use plastic, but it's a royal pain in the backside to clean.

Mix the **cilantro, chicken,** and **1 cup of the enchilada sauce** together so that they are evenly combined. The key is balance.

Dip each wonderful tortilla in the remaining enchilada sauce, fill it with **2½-3 tablespoons of filling**, and **roll them into their little _burrito_ shapes.** Place each tortilla in the pan and **repeat with the remaining tortillas** and filling until your load is ready to cook.

Spread any of your **remaining enchilada sauce over the top of the enchiladas** until you literally are salivating. **Sprinkle on top with the shredded cheese** and prepare to get your grub on!

Microwave for approximately 5-7 minutes. You'll know you're there when the cheese is completely melted, the sauce is nice and bubbly, and the enchiladas are heated all the way through.

Enchiladas!

These little guys taste so good, you'll think your microwave just became a Mexican restaurant. Luckily, it's not going to get raided by immigration every 2 weeks while republicans call you names out of one side of their mouth, while they ask you for your vote out of the other.

Enchiladas!

Roasted garlic

If any of you find yourselves with those pesky vampire issues, have no fear... Roasted garlic is here! People say, "you can't roast garlic in a microwave," but those people don't have the right technique, or they're themselves vampires.

Now, this is good technique even if you are using conventional cooking methods, because roasted garlic is a staple in many dishes. You might consider adding roasted garlic to casseroles, various pasta salads, dishes that involve your various Italian delights, fish... There are endless possibilities.

Roasted Garlic

Technically we aren't "roasting" the garlic. This process is actually steaming them, but it gives you an incredibly soft, squishy, cooked garlic that can be used anywhere. Also, this will take you 6-8 minutes instead of an hour or more, as with a conventional oven process.

Ingredients:

- 1 or more heads of raw garlic
- Virgin Olive Oil
- Sea Salt (you can use regular salt if you like raising your blood pressure)
- Pepper
- Water (or optionally *White Wine*)

Process

The **first step** in this process is to **cut the tops off of each head of garlic**, exposing the cloves to the world. Then we need to place the **garlic heads** in a **baking dish** and **lightly drizzle** with **virgin olive oil** (who doesn't love good virgin). **Sprinkle lightly** with a **tiny pinch of salt and pepper.**

Now we are going to **pour in about 1 1/2 tablespoons of water for each head of garlic** we are cooking. (Optionally: You could substitute water for white wine, for a winey-infused garlic which will kick a lot of a$$)

Roasted Garlic

Cover your cooking dish with a microwave-safe lid and **microwave at 50%** of your microwave's power in **3 minutes sessions**. After each 3 minutes, you'll need to poke the garlic with a fork to test how tender the cloves have become (*Be careful because hot garlic-flavored steam will burn your eyes if you're not paying attention and you'll be rolling around on the floor like a mindless psychopath until the pain subsides*).

Roasted Garlic

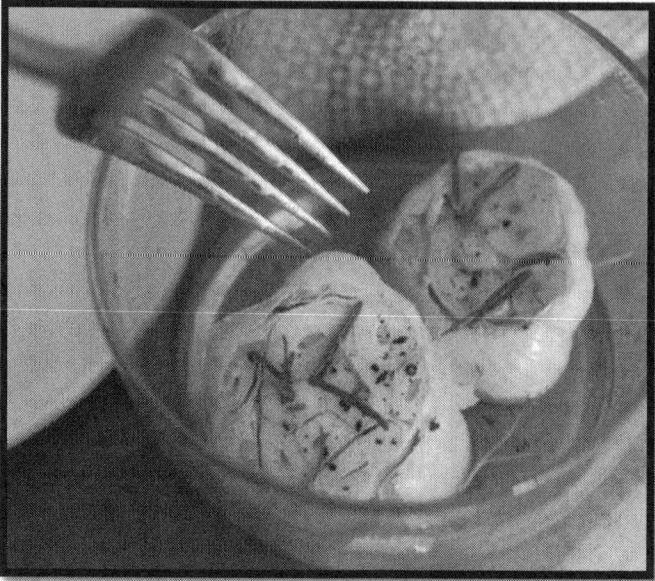

Check on the garlic after each 3-minute period, poking it with a fork to see how tender the garlic cloves have become. (*Be careful when removing the lid, again, no need to get your eyes melted twice*)

Continue with your microwave cooking, still at 50% power setting. **After 6 minutes have passed, you will reduce your cooking time to increments of 1 minute** each, until the garlic is very soft and can be easily pierced with a fork.

You could squeeze the garlic out of the cloves and use it in a recipe, eat it straight if you've got a death wish or never plan to date again, or give it a light toast in a conventional oven (or with a flame thrower).

Roasted Garlic

Quick Roast in conventional oven:

Start by heating the oven to 450°F. Wrap the steamed garlic head in a large piece of foil and place it in the baking dish (*you will need to empty out any remaining water first*). Now, bake the garlic for 10 to 15 minutes or until the garlic has begun to achieve the desired color and texture for whatever the hell it is you're adding it to.

Roasted Garlic

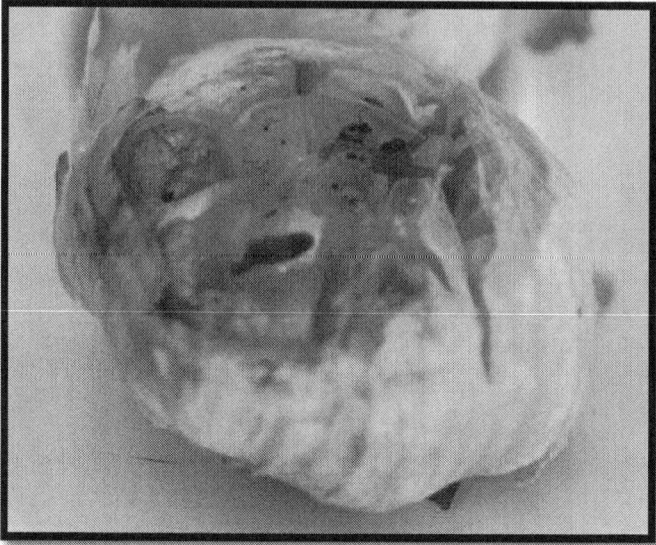

Sour cream and onion veggie chips

Feel like having a bag of chips, or just have a craving you need to satisfy...? Look no further because we have a delicious sour cream and onion vegetable chip that will taste like you bought it from the front gates of Frito-Lay!

Ingredients

- 1 potato (which needs to be thinly sliced)
- 1 Sweet Potato (which needs to be thinly sliced)
- 1 Zucchini (which needs to be, you guessed it... thinly sliced)
- 1/3 cup of powdered buttermilk
- 1 tablespoon of sea salt
- 2 tablespoons of Parmesan cheese
- 1 tablespoon of Onion Powder

Sweet Potato

- * Freshly Chopped Chives for garnish (*optional addition for flavor and variety)
- * Little spritz of cooking oil (*This is an optional step)

Process

So, the first step in creating these delicious chips is to **mix** the **powdered buttermilk,** the **sea salt,** the **Parmesan cheese** and the **onion powder together** in a **medium-sized bowl** for the **Seasoning**.

If you haven't already, please make thinly sliced "chips" from your whole vegetables.

Place each vegetable (one at a time) into a parchment lined **microwave safe plate** and spray with the **tiniest bit of oil** (you can achieve this by using a Misto, or similar device).

Sprinkle your seasonings over the sliced vegetables (either by hand or by using a mesh strainer).

Microwave on high for between four and six minutes, watching as the vegetables start to brown. They must be brown or they will not crisp up, but you don't want to burn them either, so after four minutes you will need to check every minute. You repeat this process with each vegetable until all of them have been cooked.

Sweet Potato

What are you waiting for . . . eat, man. Eat!

Sweet Potato

Sweet potatoes

Sweet potatoes are delicious already, but if we had a couple of little bits and pieces we can make a wonderful snack that tastes incredible (more like a dessert than an actual dinner item) and we can do it in a relatively quick period of time.

How quick? Well, let's say your neighbor calls because a black suburban is parked out front. We all know that means the FBI is watching your house or they are about to serve a warrant for your arrest (*yeah, yeah, I know you didn't do it and this is all set up*).

35

Sweet Potato

Anyway, while the FBI is deciding which way they are going to breach your house, you want one last snack before you're eating all of that prison food. Don't worry; you got plenty of time for sweet potato with almond butter and cinnamon.

Ingredients

1 Sweet Potato

2 tablespoons of Almond Butter

1 pinch of cinnamon

1 pinch of Brown Sugar

Process

Cook your Sweet Potato in the microwave by **wrapping it in a moist paper towel and placing it inside a microwave safe bowl**. Cooking times vary from **3 minutes to 5 minutes**, based on the size of your sweet potato. Every minute after the 3-minute mark you should be **checking the softness of the potato**.

When the desired hardness (or squishiness if you're a creep) is achieved, you **take** out your **sweet potato and cut it down the center**. Press the ends to open it up like a heart-transfer patient, and **add your almond**

Sweet Potato

butter and your pinch of brown sugar. Top it all off with your cinnamon and you're ready to enjoy.

I recommend climbing onto the roof of your house, eating your delicious sweet potato while waiting for the Feds to barge in. (*In the event of a hostage/barricade situation: Ask for a helicopter with enough fuel to get to a non-extradition country. Now, there is no such helicopter in existence, but then... they're not giving you a chopper anyway so what's the difference*).

Sweet Potato

Ropa Vieja

Did somebody steal the king's dinner plate and hide it in your microwave? This is like mixing *Shark Week*, *Taco Tuesday*, and *Cinco de Mayo* all together and topping it with f'ing greatness!

Ingredients

- 1 small onion (sliced to ¼ inches thickness)
- 3 cloves of minced Garlic
- 1 teaspoon of ground Cumin
- ¼ teaspoon of dried Oregano
- 2 tablespoons of extra-virgin olive oil
- Sea Salt
- Ground Black Pepper

Ropa Vieja!

- 14-ounce can of Crushed Tomatoes
- 1 cup of beef broth
- ½ cup of jarred Roasted Red Peppers (sliced)
- 2 tablespoons of Soy sauce
- 1 dried Bay leaf
- 1 ¼ pounds of Flank Steak (cut along the grain into 3 x 1.5" strips)
- 1/3 cup pimento-stuffed Olives (halved, preferably)
- 3 tablespoons of Cilantro (roughly chopped fresh leaves)
- Cooked Rice (ready for serving)

Process

Let's get down and dirty! Toss your garlic, onion, oregano, olive oil, cumin, ½ tablespoon of salt, and a few grinds of that black pepper into a microwave safe bowl (4-quart, hopefully). Cover the bowl with plastic wrap, and make it tight, and then cut a small slit in the center to be used as a vent for steam.

Microwave at 100% power until the onions are soft and translucent, which usually takes about four minutes. If the onions aren't cooked all the way through, cover and microwave again in 30-second increments until you can almost see through the onions.

Ropa Vieja!

Now you will add the tomatoes, red peppers, beef broth, soy sauce, bay leaf, and 1/2 tablespoon of salt and a little bit more black pepper. Stir this mixture and slowly nestle in the stake. Now you're going to tightly cover your cooking bowl with two pieces of plastic wrap, again cutting a slit in the center for steam. Microwave on high power (again, 100%) for 20 minutes.

Carefully remove the plastic wrap and stir, and then cover again with two additional sheets of plastic wrap where you will cook for an additional 20 minutes at 100% power. I feel like we are on the USS Enterprise at this point.

Uncover the bowl and let it cool for 5 minutes.

Remove the pieces of steak with a slotted spoon and place onto a cutting board. It should be relatively easy to shred. Using two forks you are going to shred the stake, then return it to the bowl and stir in your olives.

Tightly covered the bowl with plastic wrap once again, cutting a small slit in the center, and microwave at 100% power for 5 additional minutes. When the cooking is finished, let your wonderfully prepared ropa vieja sit, still covered with plastic, for about 5-7 more minutes.

You can then serve over white or brown rice depending on how crazy you're feeling!

Ropa Vieja!

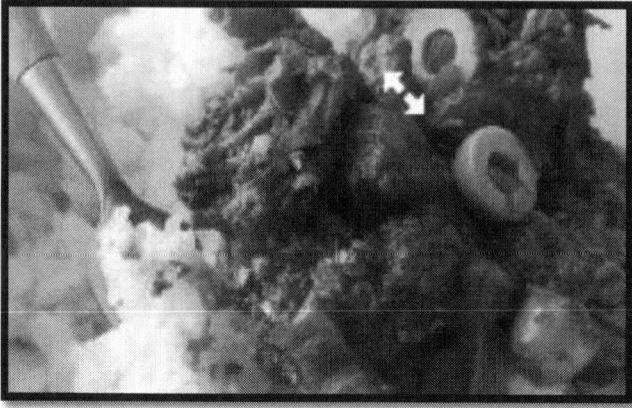

Chicken & Dumplings

We're not going to say the chicken and dumplings are the greatest meal ever created, but they're definitely in the top running. So learn this and impress even the most discerning of eaters.

Ingredients

Filling

- 2 cups of shredded rotisserie chicken (taken from ½ chicken)
- 1 cup of frozen peas and carrots
- 2 cups of low sodium chicken broth
- 1/4 cup of all-purpose flour
- 1 small-diced onion
- 1 celery stalk (sliced 1/4 inch thick)
- 2 tablespoons unsalted butter (cut into pieces)

- Sea salt
- Freshly ground black pepper
- 1 sprig of fresh thyme

Dough

- 1/2 cup all-purpose flour
- 1/4 cup of yellow cornmeal
- 1 teaspoon of baking powder
- 1/2 teaspoon of kosher or sea salt
- 1/3 cup of milk
- 2 tablespoons of vegetable oil

Process

Let's begin with the ***filling***:

We are going to whisk together the flour and chicken broth in a microwave safe baking dish (8" x 8" x 2") until there are absolutely no lumps. Once we have achieved this consistency we will stir in our onions butter, thyme, celery, ¾ of a teaspoon of salt with just a hint of pepper. Cover this entire bowl super tightly (so tight the police dogs can't smell it) with plastic wrap and cut your little slit down the middle for steam.

Microwave at full power (100%) for 5 minutes, and if your microwave is a little on the underwhelming side (say, 700-watts) then add 2 to 3 additional minutes. No more than 8 in either case.

44

Chicken Dumplings

Take the dish out of the microwave, removing the plastic wrap, and whisk the broth mixture until there are no chunks of flour in or near the bottom, then place the dish back in the microwave (leaving it uncovered) and cook at 100% power until the broth becomes bubbly and thick (which is usually 5 to 8 additional minutes).

Now for the ***dough***:

In a medium sized bowl we are going to whisk together the baking powder, cornmeal, flower, and a small bit of salt. I want you to slowly ad the vegetable oil and the milk in the center, stirring everything outward with a fork until the dough is sticky and wet.

Put it all together:

Remove the dish from the microwave, discarding your thyme sprig, and whisk this broth mixture again as you stir in the frozen peas and carrots along with the shredded chicken. You will want to form little rounded teaspoons of the dough (this recipe should make about 16 to 18 dumplings) about 1/2 inch apart along the perimeter of whichever dish or bowl you have chosen to use. Sprinkle a little bit of black pepper over each dumpling and prepare for heaven.

Cover your dish with a new piece of plastic wrap, again cutting a slit in the center, and microwave at 100% for about six minutes (checking every 30 seconds

Chicken Dumplings

after that to make sure that your dumplings are puffed to perfection). You might try using a toothpick inserted into the center of each dumpling and as you pull the toothpick out it should be clean.

Let it cool for about 5 to 7 minutes and then serve... Eat slowly and bask in the glory which you have earned as the people in the city rejoice, raising you above their heads as the people's champion!

Bravo, I dare say. Bra-vo!

Ratatouille

This meal is so delicious you will want to eat until you poop your pants, but you won't poop your pants because it is so healthy, but even if you did... You wouldn't mind because that's how delicious it is. Really a win-win in any setting!

Ingredients

- 1 medium-sized yellow onion (sliced 1/4 inch thick)
- 2 cloves of garlic (minced)
- 3 oil packed sun-dried tomatoes (chopped)
- 2 plum tomatoes (sliced into 1/4 inch thick rounds, about 8 total ounces)

Ratatouille

- 1/4 cup extra virgin olive oil
- 1 teaspoon fresh chopped thyme (about three sprigs)
- Sea salt
- Freshly ground black pepper
- 1 small eggplant (peeled and alternating stripes which have been sliced into 1/4 inch thick rounds, about 6 ounces in total)
- 1 small zucchini (sliced into 1/4 inch thick rounds, about 4 ounces total)
- 1 small yellow squash (sliced into 1/4 inch thick rounds, about 4 ounces total)

Process

Toss your garlic, sun-dried tomatoes, onion, 1 tablespoon of olive oil, 1/2 teaspoon of salt, 1/2 teaspoon of thyme, and a couple of fragments of black pepper into a microwave safe 9 inch pie dish. Use a piece of wax paper to cover the plate/dish and microwave at 100% power until the onions are soft and translucent (where you could basically see through them). Keep microwaving until there are absolutely no raw onions left, checking every 30 seconds.

Take a large bowl and place the zucchini, eggplant, and yellow squash slices along with 2 tablespoons of olive oil, the remaining 1/2 teaspoon of thyme, ½

Ratatouille

teaspoon of salt, and a few 'turns' of black pepper in. Add all of your plum tomato slices and toss very gently so as not to turn it all into a big mush ball.

While alternating vegetables, shingle the slices in a circular pattern over the cooked onions that are in the pie dish (similar to the picture above). Lightly sprinkle some of your sea salt on top and then cover with wax paper. Microwave and 100% power for about nine minutes, or until the vegetables are soft. For smaller ovens you may have to extend your cooking time out to 13 or 14 minutes. Continue to microwave, checking every 30 seconds, until there is no resistance when you pierce the vegetables using a paring knife or fork.

Once the desired softness of the vegetables is reached, we will microwave at 100% power for between three and four minutes to evaporate any excess moisture. At this point you may choose to drizzle the remaining olive oil over the top.

Take a couple of bites, then get an agent because you're about to have your own cooking television show!

Ratatouille

Macaroni & Cheese

Macaroni and Mother-luvin' cheese... this is what we're talking about, people. This is the good life. This seems like a simple enough project for your microwave to handle, but you would be surprised how many people screw this up royally.

One of the benefits to doing it yourself is that you can make a relatively healthy version so that you don't have to have a cast-iron stomach to deal with the store-bought variety of macaroni and cheese.

Ingredients:

Macaroni & Cheese

— 1/3 cup elbow macaroni (whole grain if you'd prefer)

— 1/3 cup + ¼ cup of water (some strong microwaves will necessitate a bit more water)

— 1/3 cup of shredded Cheddar Jack Cheese

— 2 tablespoons of milk

— 1 pinch of sea salt

Process

Cooking the pasta is fairly straightforward. **Place the macaroni in a microwave safe** (rather large**) bowl**. Add the water to the bowl and **microwave for 4 minutes**, then **stir**; then an **additional 1 minute**; **stir**, and **one final minute** (for a **total of 6 minutes cooking time**). If there is a little water left, don't pour it out. Leave it for the next step.

Macaroni & Cheese

Stir in your 1/3 cup of shredded Cheddar Jack Cheese (you might substitute for different varieties of Cheddar if you're feeling frisky). Return to the **microwave for another 30-45 seconds** until the cheese has melted.

Macaroni & Cheese

Stir until the cheese has completely drowned your macaronis like *Leonardo DeCaprio* in the *Titanic*. **Add a splash of milk** (2 tablespoons) and you're in heaven!

Macaroni & Cheese

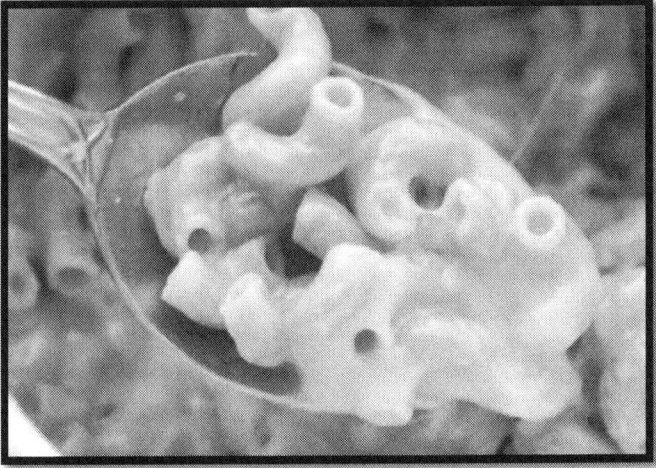

Feel like being a complete insane lunatic??? Ok, **add some bacon bits, chives** and maybe even **some diced onions**. Yeah, we just went off the hook on that one!

Macaroni & Cheese

Lemon-Horseradish Sole

We are about to warp the very fabric of space and time, undoing all of your ideas, thoughts, and conceptions about the universe with this next dish. We are going to get inside your brain box and stimulate all of your senses with this lemon-horseradish meal fit for an alien race that comes to conquer Earth.

Maybe Martha Stewart did go to prison. Just maybe she did some insider trading... but does that mean she can't cook? Hell no it doesn't. She can cook her a$$ off! And this recipe, one of her favorites, is going to prove it.

Lemon-Horseradish Sole

Ingredients

- 1 tablespoon of fresh lemon juice
- 2 teaspoons of prepared white horseradish
- 3/4 teaspoon of Dijon mustard
- 3 tablespoons of butter, softened
- 3 tablespoons of chopped fresh parsley
- 1 teaspoon of grated lemon zest
- 4 sole fillets, (at least 6 ounces each)
- Coarse Organic salt
- Lemon wedges (optionally you may elect to serve these along with the meal to really look like you know your way around a kitchen)

Process

There are only basically four steps in this process. We will start by placing our butter, lemon juice, parsley, horseradish, and mustard into a small bowl and stirring them together.

We are going to season both sides of the fillets with salt, and leave them lying open to seize fat side up) on a clean surface. You will want to keep at least 2 teaspoons butter mixture; dividing the remaining butter mixture evenly and spreading it on top of the fillets. Fold the fillets in half (in a crosswise manner) to enclose the butter mixture within the fish.

Lemon-Horseradish Sole

Place your now folded filets into a 9-inch microwave-safe dish with a tight fitting lid (plastic or glass). You should still have 2 teaspoons of the butter mixture, so now we're going to top those filets, dividing the mixture evenly. Cover the dish and then microwave at 100% power until the fish is cooked all the way through. This typically takes between 5 and 6 minutes.

When serving these fillets, place them on plates and lightly spoon out juices from the dish you just cooked in as well as garnishing with lemon wedges if you really want to be a fancy pants.

As you are eating, savor each bite and imagine Martha Stewart, dressed in her prison issued khaki pants, sitting down with a lovely group of women she met in the "yard." Nothing says family like a microwave cooked prison meal!

Lemon-Horseradish Sole

Loaded Baked Potato

There aren't too many dishes that offer the emotional support and comfort of a loaded baked potato. It's basically like having a little priest in your mouth (*which is apparently the opposite of the way it works at the Vatican*). But we digress, let's talk potatoes!

If you're ever cash-strapped, this is a cheap way to eat like a king.

Baked Potato

Ingredients:

- Russet *or* Baking Potatoes
- 2 tablespoons of Butter
- 2 tablespoons of Sour Cream
- 1 tablespoon of Bacon Bits
- 2 teaspoons of Onions or Chives
- Whatever else you dream up!

Process

Don't be a disgusting homeless person, make sure you wash the potatoes thoroughly and get off all of the toxins, pesticides, and other carcinogens that may land on it from the farm all the way to your hands.

Poke holes in your potatoes with a fork (at least four stabs will make you feel good, and you're less likely to stab the person next to you). You do not need to use a container or dish of any kind, however you should place your potatoes on a paper towel and then slide them into the microwave where you will cook on high power for 8 to 10 minutes.

Baked Potato

Carefully flip each potato and cook for an additional 10 minutes. We typically cook 3 to 4 of the larger potatoes in one microwave session, and it's never taken us more than 20 minutes for them to all feel soft to the touch.

Wearing some kind of hand protection, slice down the middle of each potato pressing the ends to expose the meat of your potato. Add your butter, followed by sour cream, and lightly sprinkle either onions or chives as well as bacon bits on top. If your religion does not allow you to eat bacon, well... that just seems like a very cruel religion to have. I guarantee you Jesus puts down a couple baked potatoes a day... just saying.

Baked Potato

And guess what . . . Jesus told me he likes cheese, lots of it, smothered all across the top of his baked potatoes. That's an absolutely true, made-up historical fact.

Salmon en Papillote

First of all, I want you guys to sound like you know your stuff when you're talking about a meal. We all know what salmon is —that super healthy fish that bears wait by the river to eat as they swim up stream. But the rest of it 'en papillote' means **in parchment paper**.

You will probably want to make this dish for no other reason than correcting people on what it means and sounding very elitist (*which is the social equivalent of spitting right in their ignorant faces*).

Anyway, this is an extremely delicious and healthy meal and it's hard to screw up, so dial this one in!

Salmon en Papillote

Ingredients

- This is definitely one of the more unique dishes we will cook. You will need 4 squares of parchment paper
- Thin sliced red potatoes
- Salmon filets
- White whine (or prison hooch)
- Sea salt
- Garlic powder

Process

Okay, let's have some fun. Layout a square of your parchment paper and take 12 small slices of red potato and lay them out as if they were fish scales in the center of your parchment paper.

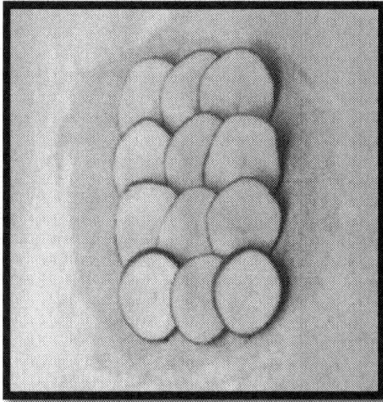

Salmon en Papillote

On top of these potato slices you'll place your salmon filet. (*The only way this could have ever happened in nature would be if a bear ate a hiker who was eating raw potato slices, then that same bear went to the river and a salmon jumped into the bear's mouth. Now here's where it gets weird . . . oh, you get it*).

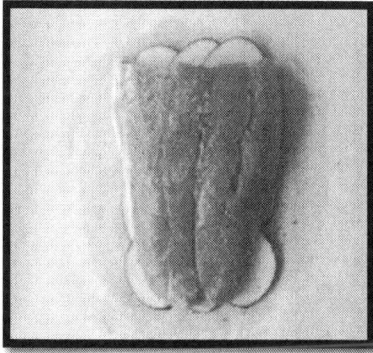

Next, top the filet with whichever herbs or spices you like (I elected garlic powder and sea salt, but you can use whatever tickles your fancy).

Salmon en Papillote

Now we are going to fold the paper the salmon but just before closing the bag I want you to add a little bit of white wine which will create a moist environment for steaming as well is to add beautiful dimensions of flavor and aroma to the dish.

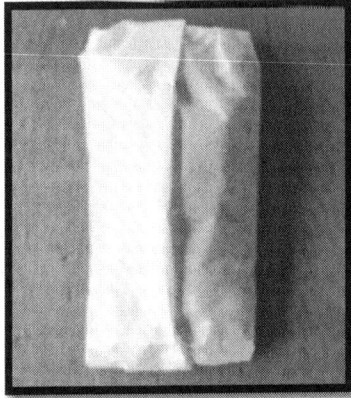

Seal the filet inside the paper and placed the entire bag (fully enclosed) in the microwave for between 3 and 3 1/2 minutes.

When done, simply unfold (or simply cut down the middle) and serve.

Salmon en Papillote

You may also serve this dish on a bed of rice or spinach. Yeah, it's that versatile!

Salmon en Papillote

Chicken Penne Al Fresco

This is just a good, delicious, hearty Italian meal cooked in a Chinese or Japanese microwave that was shipped in Russian tankers fueled by oil produced by OPEC in the Middle East. Is there any more internationally cooperative dish? I think not, sir or madam. I think not!

Ingredients:

- 4 garlic cloves (peeled)
- 2 tablespoons of dried basil
- 2 cups of Mozzarella Cheese
- 2 cups of diced, grilled chicken breasts

Chicken Penne Al Fresco

- 2 cups of cherry tomatoes
- 3 cups of uncooked penne pasta
- 4 cups of chicken broth (or 3 cups of chicken broth and 1 cup of that decadent white wine)
- 1/2 teaspoon each of salt and coarsely ground black pepper

Process

While this dish may look difficult it's actually quite simple. Spray a casserole dish with olive oil and within minutes the garlic, adding it to the dish. Now add in your tomatoes and cover the dish, microwaving at 100% four anywhere between 4 and 5 minutes, or until the tomatoes begin to burst. You should probably stir every two minutes during the cooking process.

Using the back of a spoon you will then crushed tomatoes, creating your sauce/filling. Add your pasta, chicken broth, as well as a pinch of sea salt and ground black pepper.

Cover and place the dish back in to the microwave and cook on high for between 16-19 minutes, or until the pasta is tender enough for your liking. You should be stirring after the first 10 minutes of cooking.

Chicken Penne Al Fresco

Remove your casserole dish from the microwave, removing the lid in a way that won't burn out your eye sockets. At this point you can add your chicken as well as your cheese to the dish, mixed them both very well and add in some basil.

Chicken Penne Al Fresco

Fried Rice

You can't go wrong with a dish that literally serves billions of people each day. If it's good enough for the Ming Dynasty... well then it's good enough for us! One of the great things about this dish is that it's relatively easy to prepare, it's only got about 160 calories per serving, and you can make your friends look like idiots by giving them chop sticks and expecting them to 'figure it out.'

Nothing but belly-filled laughs!

Ingredients

- 1 cup of Rice (long grain, Jasmine or Basmati)
- 1 ½ cups of water
- 1 medium Onion (chopped)
- 1 cup of vegetables (fresh or frozen, chopped)

Friend Rice

- 2 slices of bacon (chopped into little bits)
- 1 tablespoon of cooking oil
- 1 tablespoon of Soy sauce
- 1 tablespoon of tomato sauce (you can use ketchup)

Process

Place all of your ingredients into a microwave safe bowl or container; stir all of that stuff until it is a roughly uniform looking mix (all of the various colors evenly distributed). Cover with a plastic top, or plastic wrap.

Microwave and 100% power for between 18 and 20 minutes. Leave the dish, still covered, for about five minutes to soak up the rest of the moisture into the rice.

Stir, and serve to all of your guests and patrons, rocking their world!

Breakfast

Breakfast!

Egg whites and cheese breakfast sandwich

I hope you're prepared, mentally and physically for this next little treat. I know that when I'm trying to really go all-in on a breakfast meal, this is where I lay down the gauntlet! Impress your friends, the prison guards, or even your neighbors with this little breakfast miracle. The Egg White & Cheese Breakfast Sandwich. I'll let the applause settle as we begin.

Ingredients

- 1 Bagel of your choosing (use the raisin kind if you want people's minds to be blown)
- 10-15 fresh spinach leaves

Egg whites and cheese breakfast sandwich!

- ¾ cup of egg whites (which means separate out the yellow part - *you know, the chicken baby*)
- 1 wedge of crème cheese (or that yummy *Laughing Cow* cheese, pick any of their many delicious flavors)
- 2 slices of Tomato
- 3-4 slices of avocado
- 1 pinch of Sea (kosher) salt
- Hot sauce of your choosing

Process

With our bagels first, let's get them lightly browned in a toaster oven. If you haven't got a toaster oven you can be a super ninja and use an empty popcorn popping bag (*microwave use*) and center the bagel inside the bag, over the semi-metallic square thingy (*used to focus the microwave's heat by using Schrödinger's wave equations*). The bag will actually toast the bagel (or just about anything for that matter).

In a small oven safe bowl, you'll add the egg whites and spinach leaves, which you'll then lightly season with our salt. Place the bowl in the microwave for about 90 seconds (1.5 minutes), watching to make sure that the eggs don't overflow as they cook.

Egg whites and cheese breakfast sandwich!

Evenly smear your wedge of delicious cheese onto your now-toasted bagel and add slices of tomato. With a spoon, take the egg out of the microwave safe bowl as a single patty and place it over the cheese and tomato. It's getting crazy now!

Ok, you're close to perfection. Top this bad mother-lover with a couple slices of avocado, add a half-pinch more sea salt, and a splash of hot sauce (if you're not a *Nancy*).

Now sit back and enjoy the tantalizing taste bud equivalent of a thrill ride!

Egg whites and cheese breakfast sandwich!

French toast

It not possible, they said.

Two-Minute French toast is a unicorn, or a mystical dragon; it violates the laws of physics. *It just can't be done*, they told us. A scientist explained in the, queen's English, that human technology is just not advanced enough for this kind of theoretical treat.

I reminded them that people said the same of the Atom Bomb; that splitting the atom was impossible. And

FRENCH Toast!

I've got pictures of a glowing city in Japan to say otherwise.

So then those same naysayers would shake their heads, "Ok, that atom bomb thing, maybe. But 2-minute French toast . . . *never*!"

Well, ladies and gentlemen, prepare to have your mother-truckin' minds blown right out of your heads and onto your plates, because... we did it. We cracked the code.

Ingredients

- 1-2 slices of sandwich bread (per serving)
- 1 egg (per two servings)
- 1 cube of butter (per serving)
- 3 tablespoons of Milk (per serving)
- 1 pinch of cinnamon (per serving)
- 1 drop of vanilla extract (per serving)
- Syrup or Whipped Cream (as a topping)

Process

We start by cutting our bread into cute little cubes and set them to the side.

FRENCH Toast!

Then take a cube of butter and melt it into your microwave safe cup or mug. Now mix in your half egg, and milk, along with the cinnamon and a drop of vanilla extract.

Mix all of this together with a fork until it's basically uniform. Set this mixture aside for just a moment.

FRENCH Toast!

Now, place the cubes of bread gently into a separate mug, careful not to squish or jam them in. We want the liquids to slowly make their way into the bread cubes (*this occurs through differences in the pressure, as the liquid moves from a place of high concentration to one of low concentration until... never mind, you get it*).

Anyway, try and fit enough cubes to equal 1-2 slices of bread into your mug. At this point you can now pour your mixture goo into your cup of cubed bread, squishing it just a bit to let the liquid soak all the way through the bread.

FRENCH Toast!

Insert this awesomeness into the microwave and cook at 100% power for 60 seconds, then add 10-12 seconds at a time until the eggs are no longer runny.

With angels now staring at you through your windows, you'll simply add some syrup or whipped cream. This is where the press starts to pound at your door, asking for a statement, looking for pictures of your discovery, and asking for an exclusive.

Just sit back, fill your face with French toast, and laugh maniacally... one-to-nothing, *universe*. One to nothing!

FRENCH Toast!

Scrambled eggs

Scrambled eggs, people.

Did you hear what I just said? Is this mic on? I said, Scrambled freakin' eggs! Yes, they're yummy. Yes, they're nutritious. But can they be done in a microwave and not give all of your future children little flippers and oversized webbed feet... dare we say, yes?

Let's get to work!

Ingredients

- 2 eggs

Scrambled Eggs!

- 2 tablespoons of milk
- 2 tablespoons of shredded cheese (*cheddar* is our favorite, but *American* or *mozzarella* is also super yummy)
- 1 pinch of sea salt
- 1 dash of ground black pepper (and any other herbs you feel like using)

Process

This one is pretty easy. In fact, we've probably done it as a part of some of our earlier recipes. This book is so clever!

Take out your favorite microwave safe mug (12 ounce capacity) and give it a coat with some cooking spray or cooking oil (olive is the best if you have it). Crack your eggs and blend them in with milk until they're completely uniform.

Microwave this at 100% power for 45 seconds. Then stir, and cook again at 100% power for an additional 35-45 seconds, or until the eggs are just about set.

Immediately top with cheese and season this godly creation with a bit of sea salt (which is super healthy, unlike that iodized crap that cuts the insides of your arteries and releases cholesterol and raises your blood

Scrambled Eggs!

pressure, and makes doctors look at you like you can't manage your own affairs).

Oh, add a dash of pepper (red pepper is actually a nice change-up on this one) and whatever herbs or additional flavors you're after.

We have even gone so far as to add picante sauce to this dish . . . which is *caliente!*

Scrambled Eggs!

Bacon

Does bacon need an introduction?

"Bacon, this is my friend."

"Friend, meet bacon . . . we're going to eat him!"

Ingredients:

— Regular, basic, yummy uncooked bacon

Process

The key to this treat is in the paper usage. You'll want to get a microwave safe plate and place some paper towels across it. If you lay out 4 of the mini-sheets (2-3 regular sheets) that should more than do it.

Place your uncooked bacon onto the paper. You can do 1 or 2 pieces, or 5-6 at a time. No stress.

Bacon

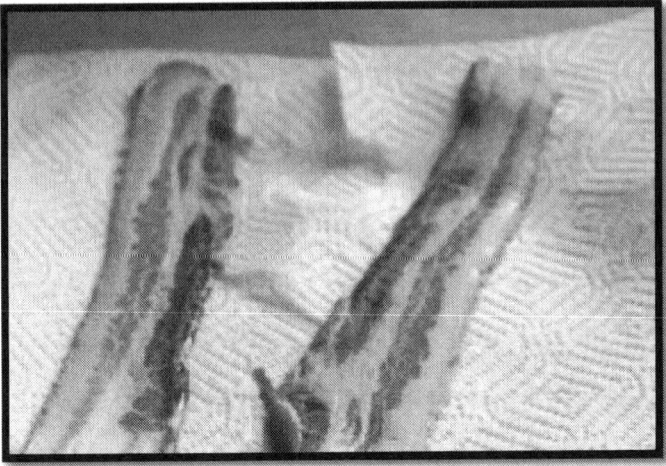

Now, fold the extra paper towel over the bacon strips you've laid out. The typical cooking time is between 90 – 120 seconds per piece of bacon. So, a typical serving of 4 slices would run you between 6-8 minutes.

After you'vè cooked, you'll actually be able to see through the paper towels because all of the grease and crap that would have clogged your arteries is now soaked up in the paper.

Bacon

Open back up the folded paper towels to reveal your delectable bacon strips, just waiting to become a part of your day. Throw away the paper, somewhere your cats won't get to...my damn cats love bacon, which is another issue altogether.

Anyway, this is a very clean way to cook your bacon and it's virtually mess free and ends up being a marginally healthier version of cooking bacon.

Bacon

Now look, if you're in the 'joint' and you don't have direct access to bacon you'll need to get several books of stamps together and figure out who you need to pay off. Likely it will be somebody who is working in the chow hall. It will probably be that chubby guy that you never see working out. Anyway, catch him on one of his breaks and make him an offer he can't refuse. Anything more than 2 books of stamps is highway robbery!

English muffins

There is always that moment in our lives when we realize we have been making mistakes since our birth. Most of these mistakes suck our time away like a tiny vampire that's stuck in your pillow at night, nibbling away your life. However, on rare occasions we can actually change the course of the future by altering our reality. Is the microwave English muffin capable of that?

Probably not.

But it tastes hella good!

Ingredients

- 2 tablespoons of canned, unsweetened pumpkin
- 2 tablespoons of Peanut Flour

English Muffin

- ½ teaspoon of baking powder
- 1 large egg (one of those badass brown ones)
- 1-2 tablespoons of milk
- 1 pinch of cinnamon
- 1 pinch of sea salt
- 1 pinch of pure sugar
- Gluten free flour (for dusting, optionally)

Process

Use a microwave safe cereal bowl and spray some cooking spray into it, adding the peanut flour and baking powder and mix until they are combined.

Now you will add in the canned pumpkin along with two egg whites or one complete egg, and mix completely until all the ingredients are evenly distributed.

Now you simply add in your cinnamon, sea salt, stir gently and place into the microwave at 100% power for between 60 and 120 seconds (2 to 4 minutes).

Remove your bowl from the microwave and dust generously with flour.

English Muffin

Now, allow your muffin(s) to cool, slice it in half, and toast it in a toaster (unless of course you don't have access to a toaster, in which case you will need to revert back to either a *microwave pizza dish*, or a *microwave popcorn bag* to facilitate the *toasting* of the muffin).

English Muffin

Mason jar pancakes

This is just a fun, cool little treat that you can make whenever the pancake urge hits you (which basically means 3 times a day for the rest of your life!).

Ingredients

-   1/3 jar of Bisquick (Bisquick pancake mix – which consists of: *6 cups of flower, 3 tablespoons of baking powder, 2 teaspoons of baking soda, and 2 teaspoons of salt*)
-   Maple syrup

Process

Without Bisquick

Mason Jar Pancakes

To make the actual pancakes with individual ingredients you'll follow these steps:

First you'll need to combine the pancake mix and the sugar in a medium-sized bowl. Beat all of it together - the buttermilk, the egg, and vegetable oil; then add this to the dry ingredients, beating the entire mass until all of the lumps are gone, and it's got a smooth, even consistency.

Pour the batter into your mason jar, but only 1/3 the way because it will expand.

Cook for between 60-90 seconds, watching closely to make sure it doesn't take over your entire microwave, then taking over your house, then gobbling up your city and become sentient, and declaring a war against all humans.

Mason Jar Pancakes

In the event that you can control this pancake's growth, let it cool for about 30 seconds and then top with maple syrup or any other delightful treat you have in mind.

With Bisquick

Follow the basic cooking process of filling your mason jar 1/3 full and then cooking for 60-90 seconds, testing after 60 seconds to test if it's cooked all the way through. To perform this test, simply insert a butter knife all the way through and then pull it back out to see if it's clean. If there are any pancake guts on the knife, it isn't ready. Place back in the microwave for another 20 seconds and check again.

Now add your toppings and fall into an ignorant, incoherent bliss that can only be matched by winning a lottery while getting a massage while being high on morphine.

Yeah, it's *that* f'ing good!

Mason Jar Pancakes

Desserts

Desserts!

Toasted Nuts

Let's be honest, who here has ever actually toasted nuts? Who does that? I've only ever seen this at carnivals, at renaissance festivals, and at this weird guy's house that lived around the corner when I was growing up and was always offering us kids cotton candy and foot massages.

Anyway, nobody toasts nuts because it's a royal pain in the butt to do it on a skillet. Well, we cracked the code on this one as well.

Ingredients

- Your favorite nuts, man.

Toasted Nuts!

Process

This is fun to say out loud, "Spread your nuts out on a plate." Ok, had to get that out there.

Evenly spread your nuts of choice on a microwave safe plate. Toast them in the microwave in 60-second intervals; stirring them and spreading them back out after each interval.

Typically, a half-cup of nuts will take about 4 minutes to toast completely. It's that flippin' easy.

One of the reasons that this recipe is so nice is that roasted nuts are a part of many different recipes, especially around the holidays, and taking up skillet or oven space is not feasible under heavy cooking conditions.

HINT: if you want these to brown a little more you can use our microwave pizza dish, or microwave popcorn bag trick. Basically, use technology to cheat the forces of the universe

Mom will be really happy that you figured this one out, unless she's in a coma. In which case, you can just sit back and relax and eat these nuts!

Baked Apples in a Bag

Why make apples in a bag?

They taste great.

They're an aphrodisiac (although not on the level of Bill Cosby or anything that potent).

They're a great addition to any other dessert you might think up! Unlike in the case of Bill Cosby, you'll actually be able to consent to eating more of them.

Ingredients

-   1 small apple (red or green doesn't matter, just whichever you prefer)

Apples in a Bag!

- 1 packet of sweetener (unless you're a man, in which case a spoonful of sugar is your answer)
- ¼ teaspoon of cinnamon
- ¼ teaspoon of cornstarch
- 1 tablespoon of water
- 1 Small handful of raisins (if you like raisins. If you don't like raisins, then this option doesn't work for you. Matter of fact, I don't really like raisins, so I'm with you on that. Try some pecans or walnuts)

Process

You may peel or not peel your apples, but you will need to take the core out and slice or dice the remaining meat of the Apple.

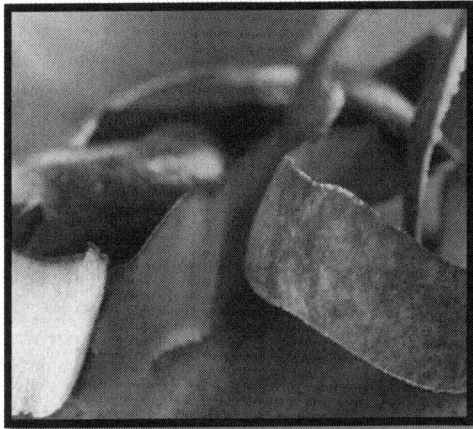

Apples in a Bag!

Get yourself a freezer quality plastic zippered bag where you are going to place the apples as well as all of your additional ingredients, and shake the living hell out of it (*marginally more than you would shake a baby if you are trying to get it to be quiet*).

Seal the bag and then reopen 1/2 inch at one of the edges to serve as a vent. Place the bag in your microwave and cook at 100% power for 2 minutes.

Wearing gloves, opened the bag very carefully and poor the contents on top of cookies, ice cream, oatmeal, Pita chips, or your grandmother's face... And enjoy!

Apples in a Bag!

'

Monkey Bread

If an angel were to chew up a golden eagle, mix it with happiness and unicorn tears, and momma-bird it back to you, Monkey Bread is what you'd be slurping down.

It's good, fluffy, fun, and easy to prepare for a big group of people at holiday gatherings... or funerals/divorce parties. So let's have some fun with this one!

Ingredients

- 1 teaspoon of vanilla
- 2 teaspoons of cinnamon
- 2 cans of biscuits
- 7 tablespoons of butter
- 2/3 cup brown sugar

Monkey Bread!

Process

So here is the plan: you're going to melt the butter and then mix it in along with the sugar, cinnamon and vanilla.

Then cut the biscuits into quarters and pour the sugary mix you just made all over it. You want to stir until the entire mass is coated sufficiently.

Place, in a microwave-safe cooking dish, into your microwave and cook at 100% power for about 4 minutes.

Let it stand for 2 minutes to cool, slip it out of the cooking dish onto another plate, and it's time go chow down!

Monkey Bread!

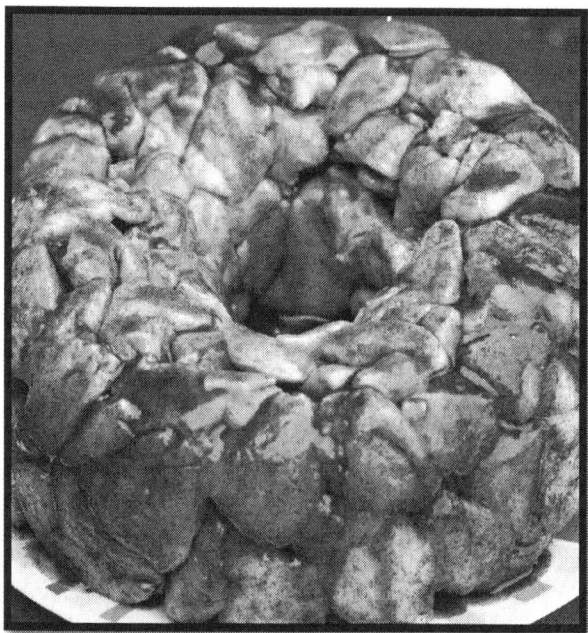

Monkey Bread!

Mug cake

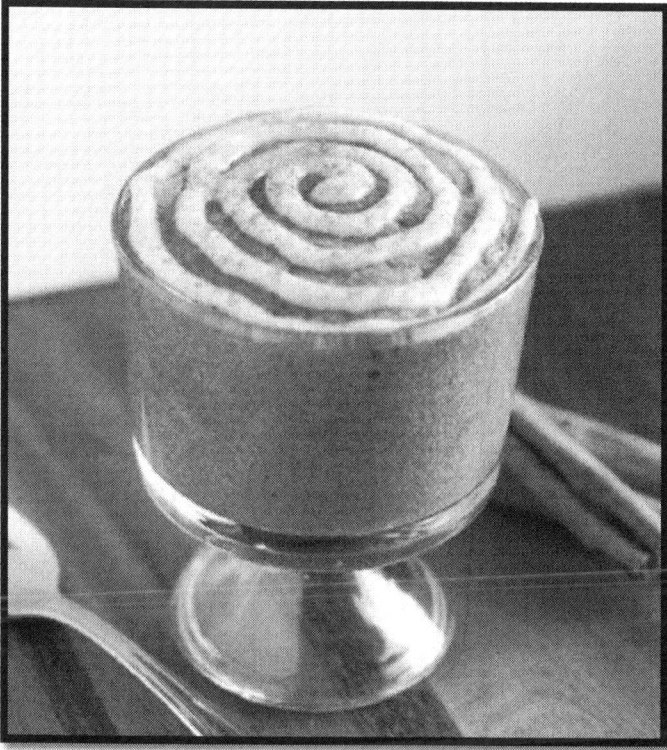

They say it only takes three minutes to get to heaven, and with this little 180-second treat I have to agree. The cinnamon roll mug cake is so good you will literally think you are eating a piece out of an angel's forearm. There are many versions and varieties of this cake, however I have chosen one that is fairly simple to re-create on a regular basis, will keep you happy, and

Cinnamon Roll Mug Cake!

keep your personal trainer employed for the next 65 years.

Lots of people think that a cake cannot be made in a microwave, but those people need to be shipped off to communist Russia because they don't know what the hell they are talking about!

Ingredients:

Icing

— 1 teaspoon of milk
— 2 tablespoons of powdered sugar
— 1 tablespoon of cream cheese (softened or whipped)

Cake

— 2 1/2 tablespoons of packed light brown sugar
— 2 tablespoons of applesauce
— 1 tablespoon vegetable oil
— 1 tablespoon of buttermilk
— 1/4 cup +1 tablespoon of all-purpose flour
— 1/4 tablespoon of vanilla extract
— 3/4 tablespoon of ground cinnamon
— 1 dash/pinch of ground nutmeg
— 1/4 tablespoon of baking powder
— 1/8 tablespoon (scanned) of salt

Cinnamon Roll Mug Cake!

Process for Icing

Ok, listen very carefully because this is going to be difficult... To make the icing you simply combine all of the ingredients into a small bowl and whisk with a fork until it is completely smooth and yummy looking. That's pretty much it.

Process for Cake

Now, there is a little bit more involved to prepare the cake itself. Combine all of your ingredients (except for your icing, obviously) into a mug and then whisk it together with a fork until it is nearly smooth.

Microwave this mixture on "high power" for 60 seconds and then check for *doneness* (which is a stupid word but it does apply). If your mixture is not fully cooked, microwave for an additional 15 seconds and give it a check... It should be ready to go.

You will serve this dish warm, with your pre-prepared icing on top. This is especially good around holidays, or funerals (which may be one in the same if your ex is a real douche bag, but I digress... Enjoy).

Cinnamon Roll Mug Cake!

Vegan Coffee Cake

What the f'k is a Vegan Coffee Cake, you say?

Well, a normal coffee cake is about 800 f'ing calories. Did you know that 3,500 calories is one pound of fat. One pound of fat is like adding a baseball-sized lump of lard to your body. That's f'ing gross, people.

But we have figured out how to do a vegan version that is just as delicious, without making you into *Jabba-the-hut.*

So let's get this feast started!

Vegan Coffee Cake!

Ingredients

- 3 tablespoons of spelt or white flour
- 1/4 teaspoon of baking powder
- 1/16 teaspoon of sea salt
- 1 tablespoon of sugar
- 1 tablespoon plus 2 teaspoons of water
- 2 teaspoon of oil or melted margarine, or applesauce
- 1/4 teaspoon of vanilla extract

For the Streusel: (If you prefer a *lot* of streusel, you can be a little piggy and double all of the following ingredients)

- 1/8 teaspoon of cinnamon
- 1 and 1/4 teaspoons of brown sugar
- 1/4 to 1/2 teaspoon of oil or melted margarine
- 1 tiny pinch of sea salt
- 2 pecan halves (walnut halves will also work)

Process

First, combine all of the dry ingredients (your batter) and mix them well. Now, add in your wet ingredients and once the goo takes on a uniform mixture you're ready.

Place this to the side for a moment while we create our streusel.

Vegan Coffee Cake!

In a small bowl, combine all of the streusel ingredients together and mix them evenly.

Using a microwave-safe mug, fill with batter, but only ½ of the way (leaving room for it to rise). Sprinkle on about 2/3 of the streusel mix, then spoon the remaining batter on top of this mound you've created.

Finally, you're going to want to sprinkle on the rest of the streusel mix and cook in your microwave at 100% power for about 60-75 seconds. After the first minute, you'll need to check for doneness every 10 seconds after that.

Add additional cooking intervals of 10-seconds if your doneness test is not positive (*unlike my last visit to the clinic, but that's another story for another book – see **How My Gay Uncle F'ed Up Christmas** on Amazon*).

Vegan Coffee Cake!

Granola

Why granola? Because it's yummy and it's got some protein, and that means we can fool ourselves into thinking it's in some way healthy . . . which it most certainly is not. But again, it tastes really good.

Sometimes you just gotta take a bite and chew it and flip somebody off who doesn't understand why you're outside, at 6:30 in the morning, in your underwear, in the middle of the street, eating granola that you cooked.

Sometimes, people just don't understand. But we don't care because we are going to make this granola in our microwave and laugh at anyone who dismisses this at insanity. We're not crazy, they are. Just keep saying that.

Ingredients

- 1/2 cup of butter
- 3/4 cup of brown sugar
- 1/4 cup of honey
- 1/4 cup of water
- 1 cup of wheat germ
- 1 cup of sunflower seeds
- 1/2 cup of coconut (I used shaved)
- 1 cup slice of almonds (you might also add 3/4 cup of pecans)
- 1/2 teaspoon of salt
- 1/2 teaspoon of cinnamon
- 3 cups of old fashioned oats
- 1 cup of bran flakes
- 1 cup of peanuts (you can also use cashews)
- 1 cup of raisins, or other dried fruit you might desire

Process

The first thing we need to do is to combine the brown sugar, honey, water, butter, salt, and cinnamon into a large glass bowl (plastic if you must). We need to microwave this at 100% power for 7-8 minutes, stirring at the 4-minute mark.

Mix in all of the remaining ingredients EXCEPT for the dried fruit (if you chose to add it). Microwave at 100% for another 4 minutes, stirring at the 2-minute mark. The granola should start to take on a golden-brownish color.

Now you can mix in that dried fruit you were supposed to throw out last week when your friends came over for the game. Mix it in thoroughly and spread all of this granola out on a cookie sheet, allowing it to cool so that when you eat it, it doesn't burn off your skin like in that Indiana Jones movie where they looked at the Arc directly. You shouldn't look at the Arc directly, we're just mere mortals.

Anyway, make sure there are no large clumps and let it cool evenly. Once cooled, you can eat, or store it in an airtight container, preparing for the next apocalypse, or whenever *Skynet* finally takes over and the machines put humanity on the 'kill list.'

Granola

Lemon bars

Time to go beast-mode on the local bake sale. These little badass snacks put the rest of the kids to shame. I actually mean the kids, themselves, not just their baked products. On the black market these Lemon bars will actually fetch a higher price than your neighbors' children. That's a true made-up fact.

So let's get cracking.

Ingredients

CRUST

- 1 cup all-purpose flour
- 3 tablespoon of powdered sugar
- 1 tablespoon of lemon zest (zest from 1 lemon)
- 6 tablespoon of butter, melted

Lemon Cake

FILLING

- 1 cup granulated sugar
- 2 tablespoon of lemon zest (zest from 2 lemons)
- 3 large eggs (at room temperature, unless you work at a nuclear power facility, then just use 74 degrees as your basis for room temperature)
- ⅓ cup of fresh lemon juice (from your previously zested lemons)
- 1 tablespoon of all-purpose flour
- ½ teaspoon of baking powder
- ¼ teaspoon of sea salt

Process

Ok, here is the plan. We need to lightly grease a 9" x 9" microwave safe baking dish or we can line a casserole dish with parchment paper (got to make sure we can get our lemon bars out after we cook them otherwise we look like idiots).

Crust

For the crust we need to whisk the flour, lemon zest, and sugar together. Then stir in our melted butter and press the crust into the dish we have prepared.

Lemon Cake

We will need to microwave at 80% power for about 3 minutes, then check the firmness of the crust. If it's not firm, heat for an additional 30 seconds, again checking the firmness. Once you're satisfied, set the plate aside.

Filling

Now, for the filling we have to beat the sugar, eggs, lemon juice and lemon zest together. Next, beat in the flour, baking powder and the sea salt, and continue beating (Pee-wee Herman style) for the next 2-3 minutes.

Pour this entire new filling over the pre-made crust and microwave at 80% power for 3 minutes. Check the filling to make sure it still has just a bit of a jiggle (not as much jiggle as Dolly Parton, but as much as Beyoncé... like a fine JELLO). Keep microwaving in 1-minute intervals if it's not Beyoncé-ready.

Let the lemon squares cool completely and then refrigerate them for at least 4 hours.

Cut the mass into squares, dust it with powdered sugar, and sprinkle any additional lemon zest on if desired.

Voila!

Lemon Cake

Peanut brittle

Why Peanut Brittle?

Because you're 'Merican and you believe in the right to be happy and eat candy that cracks your fillings at Christmas parties where you know, with 100% certainty, that Ted from accounting will get piss drunk and hit on the Boss's wife, which will be a hoot because the boss is actually a Transgender male who is waiting on his surgery date and doesn't mind at all. But Suzy from Receivables is the only one who knows this, so she's not telling Ted and he's going to be in soooo much trouble.

It's going to be awesome!

Anyway . . . Peanut brittle is good.

Peanut Brittle

Ingredients

- 1 cup of sugar
- 1 teaspoon of baking soda
- 1/2 cup light corn syrup (Karo is probably the easiest to work with)
- 1 tablespoon of butter
- 1 teaspoon of vanilla extract
- 1 cup of peanuts (I use lightly salted cocktail peanuts but then I'm marginally insane and can get away with that kind of behavior)

Process

First things first, let's combine the syrup and sugar in a microwave-safe bowl (glass is the easiest, but you may not have that at your disposal, so plastic might have to suffice). Anyway, stir the sugar and syrup. Microwave at 100% power for 5 minutes.

Now it gets yummy: we are going to add the peanuts, butter, and vanilla extract. Again, we will stir this until it's uniform. Microwave for an additional 90 seconds.

Remove the bowl from the microwave and immediately you'll need to stir in the baking soda. Without a moment's delay you want to pour the entire mixture onto parchment paper or aluminum foil where you will spread the mixture into a rectangle and let it

Peanut Brittle

cool for at least an hour. Once it's sufficiently cool it will have hardened into the 'brittle' from whence it derives its colorful name.

This stuff is like the confectioner's version of crack cocaine, so be careful not to *over* indulge and find yourself in a diabetic coma, curled up on the floor, drooling through a permanent smile that your happy muscles are locked in to.

Peanut Brittle

Chocolate peanut butter mug cake

Ok, folks . . . this $hi# just got *real*! That's right, I'm talking about a Chocolate Peanut Butter Freakin' Mug Cake. Pow! The key to this little **5-minute treat** is the peanut butter, in my opinion.

Ingredients:

Peanut Butter Pie Mouse (on top)

   — 2 tablespoons of whipped cream or cool whip

Peanut Butter Mug Cake

— 1 tablespoon of powdered sugar
— 1 tablespoon of softened cream cheese
— 1 tablespoon of peanut butter
— 1/2 teaspoon of vanilla (vanilla extract)

Process for Mousse Topping

The first step in creating our mousse topping is to **mix the cream cheese, peanut butter, and vanilla together**. Then you are going to **fold in the whipped cream**, and **gently sift in the powdered sugar**. The key is **not to over stir** this mixture because you want to leave it light and fluffy.

Mug Cake

— 1 egg
— 2 tablespoons of sugar
— 2 tablespoons of flour
— 3 tablespoons of cocoa powder
— 2 tablespoons of butter
— 2 tablespoons of peanut butter
— 1/2 teaspoon of vanilla
— 1/8 teaspoon of salt
— 1/8 teaspoon of baking powder
— 3 tablespoons of chocolate chips

Peanut Butter Mug Cake

Process for Cake

We need to make our Peanut Butter Mixture up front, so our first step in creating this incredible confection is to **melt 2 tablespoons of butter into a small dish**. At this point you will **start adding the peanut butter** and mixing it **into the melting butter along with vanilla, 1 egg, and 2 tablespoons of sugar** until the entire mass is uniform.

Now, in a **separate dish, you will combine 2 tablespoons of flour, 1/8 tablespoon of salt, 3 tablespoons of cocoa powder, 3 tablespoons chocolate chips, 1/8 teaspoon of baking powder** and combine all of this into our original mug... mixing in the uniform goo that we created in our first step (the peanut butter mixture).

Time to hit the microwave: you are going to be cooking from **1 to 2 minutes** (60-120 seconds), but I urge you to start testing around the **one-minute mark**.

Peanut Butter Mug Cake

Now we can top this delicious fellow with our peanut butter mousse and some hot fudge (there are a ton of different hot fudge toppings you can get, but the original Hershey's is my favorite).

Peanut Butter Mug Cake

Peanut Butter Mug Cake

Chocolate Chip Cookies

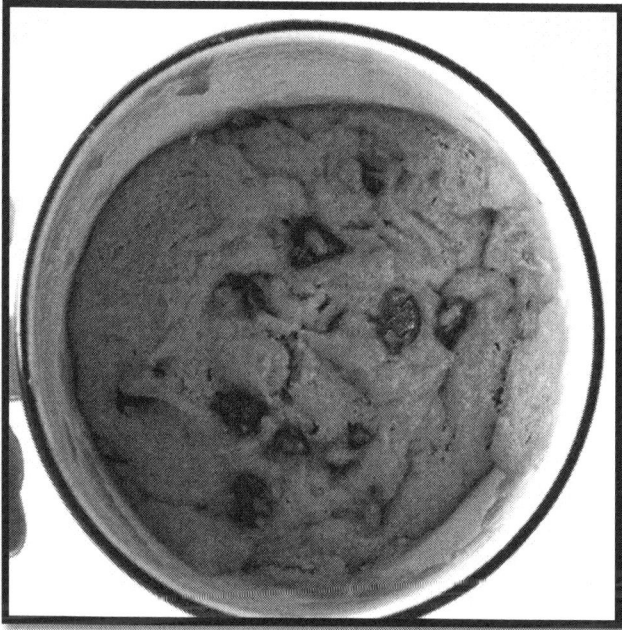

We 'bout to get crunk up in here! Chocolate chip cookie crunk (*cookie+drunk = crunk!*) that is.

If you want to eat a treat so delicious that you feel like Willy Wonka actually lives in your microwave, this is the treat for you. Who doesn't love chocolate chip cookies? Even war criminals from the Russian red Army deep in the Communist hills of the former Soviet Union love chocolate chip cookies. We do to.

This is a recipe that can be prepared in a few quick minutes and everyone who is not allergic to chocolate will enjoy this (and even the people who are allergic would at least enjoy it up until the point where they are curled up in the fetal position going into anaphylactic shock).

Ingredients:

Essential/Basic Recipe

— 1 tablespoon of real Butter
— 1 tablespoon of Granulated or organic sugar
— 1 tablespoon of Brown Sugar/ organic brown sugar
— 3 drops of Vanilla Extract
— 1 egg yolk (you won't need the egg whites for this dish, eat them because they're healthy, though)
— 1 small pinch of sea salt (super small)
— *Slightly less than* ¼ cup of All Purpose Flour
— 2 heaping tablespoons of Semi-Sweet Chocolate Chips

Different Varieties/Options

Walnuts/M&Ms/Peanuts

— Walnuts
— M&Ms
— Peanuts
— Or wherever your sweet tooth takes you!

Chocolate Chip Cookies

Process

Start, as we always do, by **melting your butter in a small dish** in the microwave. Make sure your butter is not boiling, simply melted to liquid.

Add sugars, vanilla and your pinch of salt as you stir to combine everything. It's about to smell really good up in your kitchen.

Separate your egg (removing the egg white) and add only the yolk to your cup. Stir the ingredients together as this bad boy takes shape!

Now you will **add your flower as you continue to stir**. You will want to use **slightly less than 1/4 cup of the flower**.

Now, without nibbling too many of them... pour in your chocolate chips as you stir. Your mixture has now taken on the consistency of cookie dough. Bam!

If you want to add in your additional options (Walnuts, M&Ms, or Peanuts) you'll do that at the same time you are adding your chocolate chips.

You'll then cook in your microwave oven for between 45-60 seconds. At the 45 second mark you'll need to check and see how close the cookie is to being completely cooked. A good rule of thumb is to check at

Chocolate Chip Cookies

45 seconds, then 55 seconds. Don't go past a minute, because it will be a melted burnt mess at that point.

Cookies continue to cook as they cool, so it will harden considerably if you go past one minute. You're always safe at 50 seconds.

Serve them with a glass of milk, unless you're lactose intolerant. In that case you should serve with a pair of adult diapers... and just sit back and let it all go.

Additional Book List

At Surreal.Media we publish a variety of authors in both fiction and non-fiction, all across the map. We believe that everyone deserves a voice. If you have interesting ideas, stories, or perhaps even your own book, don't hesitate to give us a jingle:

todd@surreal.media

This is a list of some of the interesting titles that Surreal.Media has published thus far, even those where he worked with Jonathan Greene, Larry Ward, Jayden Huck, Jill Falter, Nicholas Black & Stephanie King:

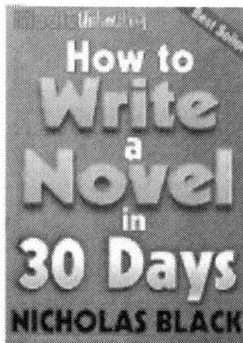

1. **How to Write a Novel**: How to Write a Book in 30 Days - Write an Amazon Kindle Best Seller in Less than 1 Hour...

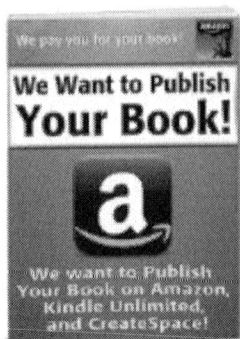

2. We Want to Publish Your Book!: We want to Publish Your Book on Amazon, Kindle Unlimited, and CreateSpace!

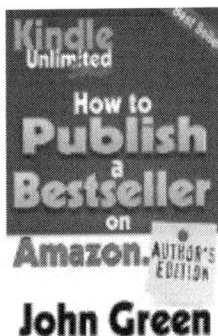

3. **How to Publish a BEST SELLER on Amazon.com:** Kindle Unlimited Author's Guide to Publishing a Book on Amazon (Kindle...

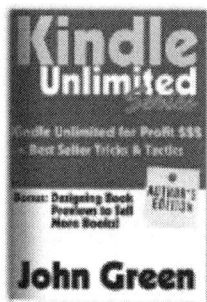

4. **Kindle Unlimited**: Everything there is to know about the Kindle Unlimited Subscription + 100 Kindle Unlimited ebooks...

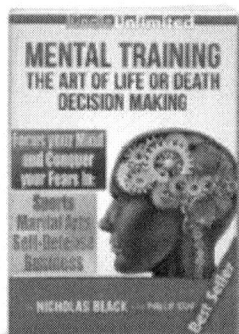

5. **Mental Training**: The Art of Life or Death Decision Making - How to Conquer fear in Sports, Martial Arts, Self...

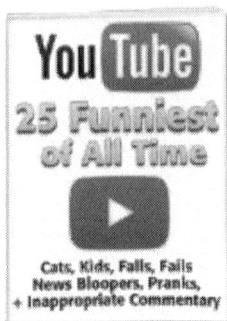

6. YouTube: The 25 Funniest Videos of All Time (Cats, Kids, Falls, Fails, News Bloopers and Inappropriate Commentary...

7. **Whispy**: The Cloud who Lost his Lightning (Unlimited Freetime Kids Books Series Book 1)

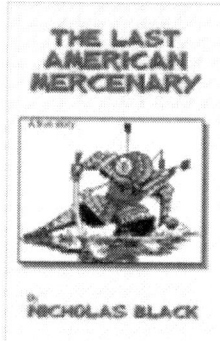

8. **The Last American Mercenary:** The true story of an average guy who ended up as a mercenary!

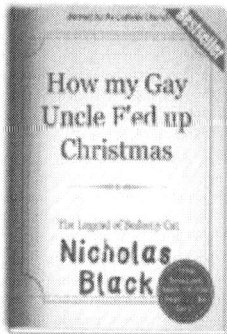

9. **How my Gay Uncle F'ed up Christmas**: The Legend of Sodomy Cat (Kindle Unlimited Exclusives by Nicholas Black)

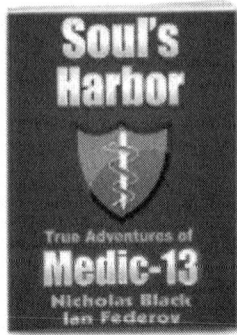

10. **Soul's Harbor**: True Adventures of Medic-13 - Kindle Unlimited Exclusive (Kindle Unlimited Series by Nicholas Black)

11. **Purg I:** Fallen Angel: Purgatory Series, Part 1 - Paranormal Romance - Thriller - Suspense (Purg Series)

Additional Interesting Reads

12. **Purg II**: The 4th Angel: Purgatory Series Part 2 - Paranornal - Science Fiction - Thriller (Purg Series)

13. **Purg III**: Burning Heaven: Purgatory Series Part 3 - Paranornal - Science Fiction - Thriller (Purg Series)

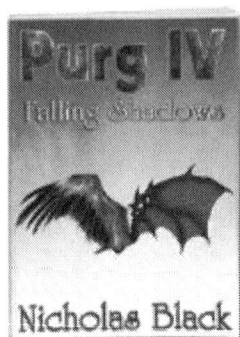

14. **Purg IV:** Falling Shadows: Purgatory Series Part 4 - Paranornal - Science Fiction - Thriller (Purg Series)

15. **See Jack Die:** Paranormal Thriller (See Jack Die Series Book 1)

16. **See Jack Hunt**: Paranormal Romance - See Jack Die Part 2 (See Jack Die Series)

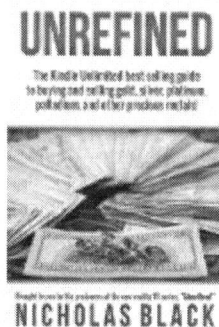

17. **"Unrefined"**: The Unlimited best selling guide to buying and selling gold, silver, platinum, palladium, and other...

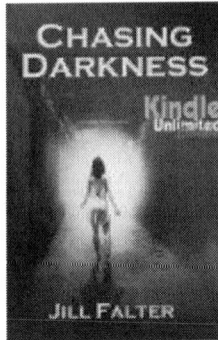

18. **Chasing Darkness**: Paranormal Romance - Chasing Darkness Part 1 (Chasing Darkness Paranormal Romance Series)

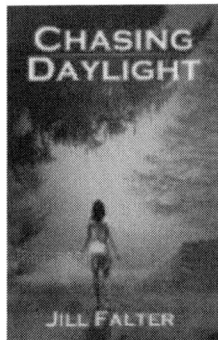

19. **Chasing Daylight:** Paranormal Romance - Chasing Darkness Part 2 (Chasing Darkness Unlimited Series)

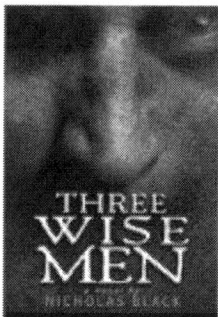

20. **Three Wise Men:** Suspense - Thriller (Kindle ebooks by Nicholas Black Book 4)

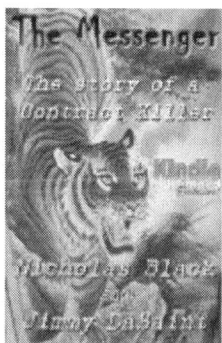

21. **The Messenger**: The Story of a Contract Killer: Urban Fiction (Urban Fiction by Nicholas Black Book 1)

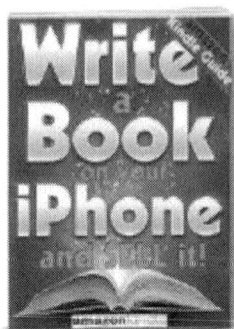

22. **iPhone 6 Writer's Guide**: Write a Book on your iPhone and Sell it - Amazon Kindle Guide (Kindle Unlimited Success...

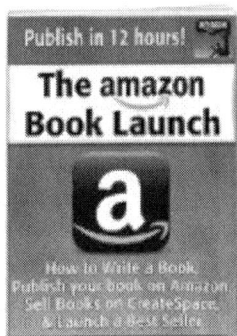

23. **The Amazon Book Launch**: How to Write a Book, Publish the book on Amazon, Sell Paperbacks through CreateSpace,...

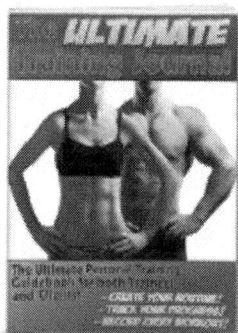

24. **The Ultimate Training Journal**: The Ultimate Personal Training Guidebook for both Trainers and Clients (Create...

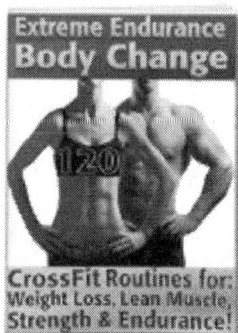

25. **Extreme Endurance Body Change**: 120 CrossFit Routines Designed for Weight Loss, Lean Muscle, Strength and Endurance...

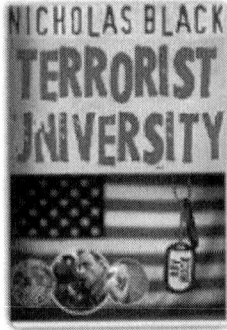

26. **Terrorist University:** Understanding Terrorism, ISIS, Al Qaeda, Terrorist Attacks and the Mindset of the Insurgent...

27. **Credit:** How to Fix Your Credit: Unlimited Guide to - Credit Score, Credit cards, Credit Repair Secrets, debt and...

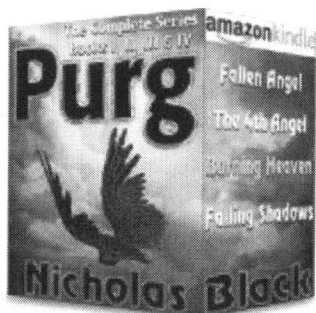

28. **Paranormal:**

PURG - The COMPLETE PURGATORY SERIES of 4 Paranormal Thriller-Romance Books: Fallen Angel, The 4th...

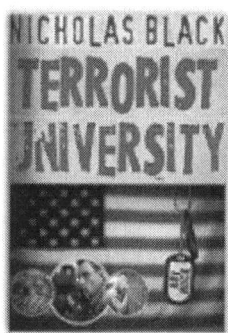

29. Terrorist University: Understanding Terrorism, ISIS, Al Qaeda, Terrorist Attacks and the Mindset of the Insurgent...

32417033R00108

Made in the USA
Middletown, DE
04 June 2016